GREAT
BRITISH
RAILWAY
JOURNEYS

GREAT BRITISH RAILWAY JOURNEYS

CHARLIE BUNCE

Collins

First published in 2011 by Collins

HarperCollins Publishers
77-85 Fulham Palace Road
London W6 8JB

www.harpercollins.co.uk

13 12 11
9 8 7 6 5 4 3 2 1

Text © Charlie Bunce 2011

Charlie Bunce asserts his moral right to be identified as the author of this work.

Design by Fivebargate.
Picture research by Amanda Russell.

A catalogue record for this book is available from the British Library.

ISBN: 978-0-00-739476-0

Printed and bound in Italy by L.E.G.O. S.p.A.

For Scarlett and Tallulah,
the light at the end of my every tunnel

ACKNOWLEDGEMENTS

It has been a great privilege to work with the amazingly talented
team responsible for *Great British Railway Journeys*. Thank you all.
Special thanks to Michael Portillo and producer extraordinaire Fiona
Caldwell, who helped me shape the series. Together we decided what
routes to take, where we should stop, and what to do once we got
there; together we wrote the scripts that have gone on to become the
backbone of the book. Thank you too to Marc Beers, Chloe Sarfaty,
Rob Daly, Laura Donaghey, Tim Brocklehurst and Colin Rothbart
who, despite being the least likely band of train enthusiasts you are
ever likely to come across, have spent many months filming Michael as
he criss-crossed the country by rail. They are the 'we' in this book, and
I am in awe of them.

Four books were invaluable in researching the series and book: *A
Historical Dictionary of the Railways in the British Isles* by David Wragg;
Fire and Steam by Christian Wolmar; *The Victorian Railway* by Jack
Simmons; and *Consuming Passions* by Judith Flanders.

Special thanks to Liam Keelan and Pam Cavannagh at the BBC: Liam
for his clear vision and help as we worked out what the programme was;
Pam for keeping us on track through the second series.

Thank you to Karen Farrington and Cat Ledger who in very
different ways kept my head above water whilst I was trying to write
the book. Also to Helena Nicholls, Steve Burdett and Steve Dobell at
HarperCollins, Giorgia Papapietro for finding many of the wonderful
photographs and Rhiannon MacDonald for her relentless fact checking.

Thank you always to Corinne.

Last but never least, thank you to Camilla Lewis for asking me to
produce the programme and suggesting I write the book.

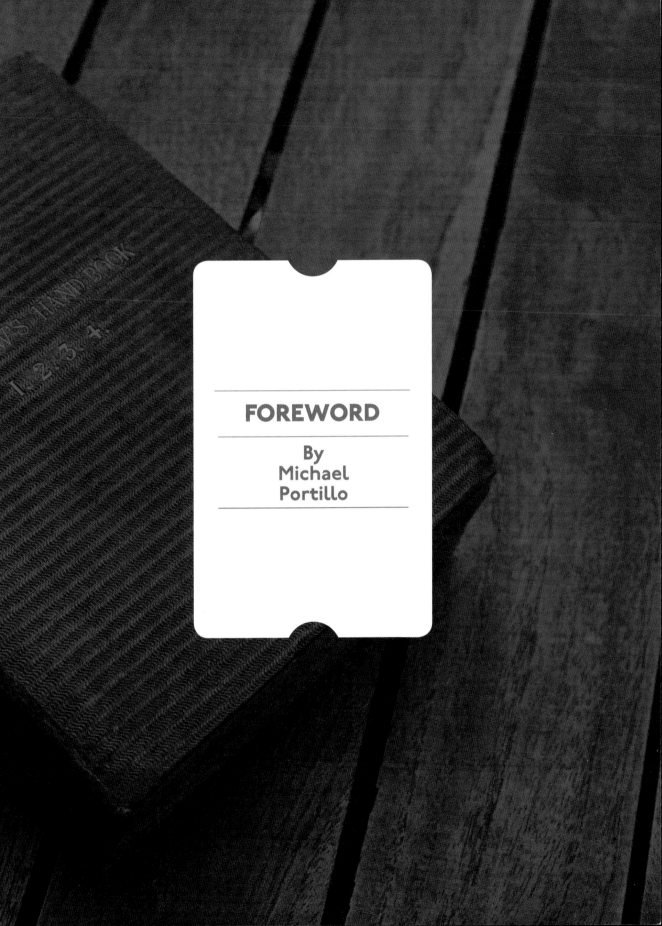

FOREWORD

By
Michael
Portillo

Like most people, I thought travel an adventure when I was a child, and most of those adventures were by train. There were still some steam trains around for me. There was a tank engine-hauled service from Belmont to Harrow and Wealdstone, close to where I grew up. My eldest brother, Charles, would take me on the 'Belmont Rattler', and I remember the panting engine, the smoke and my excitement.

For summer holidays we would go to the Isle of Wight by electric train from Waterloo, but from Ryde we would pick up the steam service along the island's east coast. The tunnel beneath the Boniface Downs would fill with the pungent stench of steam locomotive just before we pulled into Ventnor.

Then there was the annual excursion to my mother's hometown of Kirkcaldy. My parents were not well off, so we took the overnight train without sleeper reservations, travelling second class, sitting upright, sustained by Lucozade and peanut butter sandwiches. On at least one occasion it took 13 hours, and the service was known, to our sardonic amusement even then, as the Starlight Special.

After childhood, trains became mere tools for me. As a politician I visited most places to campaign, cut a ribbon or make a speech. The train got me there, or got me there late. The glamour was gone, and I was all too ready to criticise the lateness, the absence of the refreshment trolley or the failure of the air conditioning.

Now I find myself drawn to the railways once again. Making the two series of Great British Railway Journeys has meant spending almost 100 days travelling the length and breadth of the country and has brought back for me the idea of railway journey as adventure. Catching the train has been a key part of the experience, not merely a chore.

I was always travelling to see. I journeyed with curiosity and optimism, and I was rarely disappointed.

My guide was a Victorian called George Bradshaw. In 1839 he started producing railway timetables and then a handbook to journeying through Britain by train. Even though I have travelled most of the routes before, this book shone an endlessly fascinating light on everywhere I visited. I have studied the Victorian period at school and university, but no document that I have read before is quite as revealing of the Victorian outlook as this travel guide.

FORMER MINISTER MICHAEL PORTILLO REVISITS HIS LOVE OF RAILWAYS.

Bradshaw's generation was highly excited by its central role in a world that was moving forward at an exhilarating pace. His wonder and pride spill from every page. Enthusiastic, patriotic, opinionated, he writes in an era unrestrained by egalitarianism, let alone political correctness. His age values reason, experimentation and excellence. It is serious and largely unsentimental. For Bradshaw there was no shame in imperialism, no consideration of taste to restrain his bombast. Manchester manufacturers, he records with pride, could import the cotton crop from India, spin it and export textiles that would then undercut local production in India. London, he says, is the greatest city that exists, or has ever existed. He is right that London stood at the heart of an empire that exceeded that of the Pharaohs or Caesars, and considering Britain's mastery of technology there was no serious competition to be found anywhere in the world's history.

Bradshaw's first enthusiasm was for canals, a prodigious achievement in themselves with a great impact on business. But the railways were faster and more versatile. Above all they were for the masses. Without large numbers of passengers they were uneconomic. They altered the geography of Britain by making places accessible, and they transformed the social landscape because people of modest means could travel.

The speed of the change is difficult even for us to grasp, because although the mobile phone and computer have led to a revolution over the last 20 years, modern-day Britain doesn't undergo physical change as fast as Victorian Britain did. The world's first intercity line opened between Liverpool and Manchester in 1830. Twenty years later over 6,000 miles of track had been laid, reaching all but the remotest parts of the country. Railways sprang up everywhere. Some important lines were built in their entirety in just two years. Although steam engines were used in construction, most of the work was done by hand. Thousands of navvies occupied camps along the route, and dug the cuttings and raised up the stones for the viaducts. We would have to visit modern Shanghai, perhaps, to gain any understanding of the speed of change and the scale of the undertaking.

The handbook's itineraries follow the tracks. Towns are listed not alphabetically but in their order along the main lines and branch lines. I have been asked a lot whether I didn't find that many of Bradshaw's routes have gone. Some have, of course. But I think I was more struck but the degree of continuity between then and now. Britain today, despite its post-war motorways, depends upon an infrastructure laid down by the Victorians. They built to last, and often grandly. As the refurbishment of St Pancras has shown, the best thing to be done with a Victorian building is simply to undo the damage of decades caused by smoke and rain and, particularly, cheapskate makeovers. Stand on Waterloo Bridge with Bradshaw's book and you may find that the finest buildings today are still the ones that he picked out: Saint Paul's cathedral, Somerset House and Parliament.

That gives a clue as to why travelling with Bradshaw is still useful today. Not to despise the work of later generations, but to appreciate the magnificent and formative legacy of that era. It led me to explore places that are no longer in fashion, like Scarborough and Weston-super-Mare, and to hunt for trades that were big in his day, like Walsall saddlers, Bristol glass blowers and Denton hatters.

I never intended my journeys to be purely nostalgic, and they have not been. British cities are rejuvenating themselves and British resorts cling on or fight back. There is vibrancy and enthusiasm wherever I have been. The Britain of today would be ethnically, culturally and socially unrecognisable to George Bradshaw. I hope that in my journeys I portray Britain as it is.

Michael Portillo
2010

INTRODUCTION

By
Charlie
Bunce

There are some ideas for television programmes that, when you hear about them, you just know in your bones are destined for success. That was certainly the case when I was asked to produce a new series being developed for the BBC which was then called *Adventures with Bradshaw*.

The idea emerged from a brainstorming session with Liam Keelan, BBC Controller of Daytime and Camilla Lewis, Head of Factual Features at talkbackTHAMES. Liam was keen to find a programme that would work at 6.30 p.m. on BBC2. He wanted a travelogue by train, which had an historical angle. Liam knew the railways were rolling out across Britain during one of the most exciting and rapidly advancing periods of history when ordinary lives were being irrevocably changed.

Camilla had long been obsessed with finding a new way of investigating our social history. Her brother-in-law, an antiquarian bookseller slotted the last piece of the puzzle in place when he told her that George Bradshaw, the man who famously started producing monthly railway timetables in the mid-nineteenth century had also published a guide-book on travelling across the country by train.

After a £500 investment, a battered and broken copy of Bradshaw's guide arrived at the office. A drab brown cover was misleading as its contents were anything but dull and dreary. Its well-thumbed pages offered a remarkable insight into the life and times of Victorian Britain.

The more I read Bradshaw's guide, the more I could hear his voice. As I understood him better I began to see the age in which he lived and worked, and to see what excited him and why. His minute observations and comments gave me a sense of Victorian Britain different from anything I'd read before.

His rich words conveyed to us another age. A section about Sandwich in Kent is an ideal example. 'The traveller, on entering this place, beholds himself in a sort of Kentish Herculaneum, a town of the martial dead. He gazes around him and looks upon the streets and edifices of a bygone age. He stares up at the beetling stories of the old pent-up buildings as he walks and peers curiously through latticed windows into the vast low-roofed, heavy-beamed, oak-panelled rooms of days he has read of in old plays.'

How could you not want to visit Sandwich and find what he had seen. Beyond lyrical descriptions, Bradshaw deposited on his pages a wealth of information about where his readers should stay, how to get money, what day the market took place, local sights of interest and on occasion where

GEORGE BRADSHAW COMBINED HIS ENTHUSIASM FOR CARTOGRAPHY WITH A PASSION FOR TRAINS.

to sit to get the best view from the train. He revelled in detail, giving the span and height of bridges to the foot, or the length of station platforms. He loudly and proudly celebrated every British success.

Bradshaw described how the railways were a great leveller, literally and metaphorically. While the land was planed so the trains could run on as few inclines as possible, the barriers that divided a class-ridden society were at the same time pared down.

For the enterprising, railways represented a golden opportunity. Although they were initially seen as a way of transporting freight, it wasn't long before moving people by rail was just as important, sometimes even more so. Commerce spread across neighbourhoods and regions. Trades that were once restricted to narrow localities could now take advantage of markets worldwide. The notion of commuting was born. Holidays, once the province of the rich, came within grasp of ordinary people.

It is difficult to imagine now just how fundamentally life changed and the speed at which those transformations came about. Where railway stations were made, hamlets mushroomed into towns while those settlements that were leapfrogged by railway lines were left in the doldrums.

BRADSHAW WAS AN EXPERT ARTIST, AND HIS LINE DRAWINGS OF SOME OF THE COUNTRY'S FINEST BUILDINGS WERE INCLUDED IN HIS POPULAR GUIDEBOOKS.

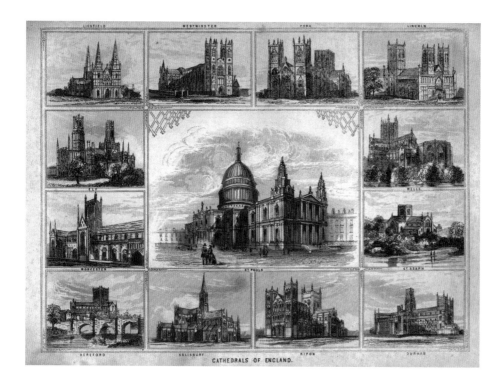

CATHEDRALS OF ENGLAND.

It wasn't all good news, though. Amid the euphoria that accompanied the age of steam there were many who fell victim to railway mania, including those who died laying tracks in hostile terrain and the unwary who invested heavily in lines or companies that failed to flourish.

As far as the programme was concerned, the idea was beguilingly simple. We would travel Britain by train with Bradshaw as our guide. Through it, we'd explore the impact of the railways on our cities, countryside and coast. Thanks to Bradshaw, we could celebrate triumphs of yesteryear and match fortunes past and present. We would see how the country had been transformed in a matter of a few short years and understand why, at the time, the British Empire was so successful at home and overseas. But, as importantly, we would search out what of Bradshaw's Britain still remains today.

The next question was who should present it. In television, getting this agreed is often a monumental feat. On this occasion it wasn't. Michael was suggested, and within 30 seconds of meeting him I knew he was the perfect candidate. The son of a Spanish refugee and a Scottish mother, Michael not only had a lifelong fascination for history but was also a

BELOW: **LONDON LANDMARKS WERE ALSO ILLUSTRATED BY BRADSHAW FOR VISITORS TO THE CAPITAL.**

OVERLEAF: **MICHAEL PORTILLO SPOKE WITH FELLOW RAILWAY ENTHUSIASTS UP AND DOWN THE COUNTRY – HERE WITH IAN GLEDHILL, CHAIRMAN OF VOLK'S ELECTRIC RAILWAY ASSOCIATION.**

1883

Last Train Tonight

5pm

Health & Safety

Pushchairs...

must be folded
stowed correctly
re the train depart

a safe day.

former Minister of Transport. Years spent in both government and opposition did nothing to diminish his abiding passion for railway journeys. Forty-five episodes later I have never once regretted the decision to have him present the show. The energy and intelligence he brings to every situation make the series stand out.

Strangely, the most taxing bit of the whole process was coming up with the right title. List after list was emailed to everyone concerned with the project, only to be knocked back, judged not quite right. We must have gone through hundreds of suggestions before ending up with *Great British Railway Journeys*. In the end, it seemed to say very succinctly what the series is all about.

The last question was where those journeys should take us. We could not mimic Bradshaw minutely on our travels. His extraordinary thoroughness meant that was a task too far, and many of the stations he visited are now obsolete, thanks to the policies of the Sixties which saw thousands of miles of branch lines closed in a futile bid to save cash.

Nonetheless, I wanted the trips we recorded to reveal a country that many of us hardly know, or at least seem to have forgotten. With our copy of Bradshaw's guide in hand we've now made nine big journeys exploring the country and discovering new sides to places I thought I knew well. Through making the programmes and writing the book, I have had the chance to tease out dusty nuggets of information to satisfy the most curious of minds. I wanted the chance to trumpet what had been great about Britain, and celebrate the enormous amount that still is. I hope the series and this book do just that.

Charlie Bunce
September 2010

AS HE TRAVELLED THROUGH BRITAIN MICHAEL PORTILLO KEPT HIS WELL-WORN COPY OF BRADSHAW'S RAILWAY GUIDE CLOSE AT HAND.

JOURNEY

1

COTTONOPOLIS AND THE RAILWAYS

From Liverpool to Scarborough

The obvious place to start our journeys seemed to be the birthplace of the modern passenger railway. Lots of places lay claim to that title, but for us, once we'd looked into it, the Liverpool & Manchester Railway was the clear winner. It is true that fare-paying passengers had been carried by rail before its inception, but the Liverpool & Manchester was different. Unlike the other railways that predated this one, carriages were not horse-drawn, nor were they pulled along wires fixed to a stationary locomotive. It wasn't a tiny pleasure railway with limited use. This was a proper twin-track line, the first in the world where steam locomotives hauled paying passengers, and it changed the face of travelling in Britain.

There are certainly longer, older and more beautiful routes, but the line between Liverpool and Manchester seemed to us to be the perfect launch pad into the past.

The original purpose of the line wasn't to service passengers at all, but to move freight between two booming cities. At the beginning of the nineteenth century, most goods were transported on a thriving and extensive canal system, but it was both expensive and slow, and this trip took 36 hours. So in 1822 Joseph Sandars, a local corn merchant and something of a forward thinker, decided to invest £300 of his own money in surveying a route for a railway between Liverpool and Manchester.

The project suffered numerous setbacks as aristocratic local landowners campaigned to prevent the proposed line from passing through their lands, while the canal owners, fearful of competition, tried to stop it altogether. It looked for a while as though it would never get off the ground until another blow turned out to be the line's saving grace. When the project's original surveyor landed himself in jail, George Stephenson (1781–1858) was appointed in his place.

Stephenson was one of those great Victorians for whom nothing seemed impossible. Born to parents who could neither read nor write, he went on to become an inventor, a civil engineer and a mechanical engineer. He designed steam engines, bridges, tunnels and rail tracks. Whilst there's disagreement over whether his skills lay in invention or in harnessing other people's creations, he is rightly known as the father of the railway. Without a doubt, the modern railway developed more quickly than it would have done without Stephenson's involvement.

On the line for the Liverpool & Manchester Railway, one of the first things Stephenson was tasked with was re-examining the route. What

ENGINEER GEORGE STEPHENSON IS CONSIDERED THE FATHER OF THE RAILWAYS.

he came up with was a new plan which as much as possible skirted contested land. In this instance it wasn't an easy option. It would require building no fewer than 64 bridges and viaducts along its 35-mile course and needed Parliamentary permission before it could begin.

It took four years of haggling before the Parliamentary Bill was passed in May 1826, enabling the compulsory purchase of land for the railway. Getting to this point had cost many compromises, however, one of which was that the line couldn't go into Liverpool itself and instead had to halt outside the city centre. After the opening of the line in 1830 it was a further decade before it could be extended into the city and Lime Street station, one of Britain's first railway stations, was opened.

In the middle of the nineteenth century Manchester was the centre of the cotton industry and Liverpool was a bustling dockyard. In fact, Bradshaw's *Descriptive Railway Hand-Book*, the Victorian railway bible that we used throughout our travels around Britain, hails Manchester as 'sending its goods to every corner of the world'. Liverpool had the port to facilitate doing just that. Bradshaw calls the docks 'the grand lions of the town which extend in one magnificent range of five miles along the river from Toxteth Park to Kirkdale'. By 1850 – just 20 years after the Liverpool & Manchester line opened – Liverpool docks were the second most important port in Britain, handling 2 million tons of raw cotton every year destined for the Lancashire mills.

For Liverpool, it wasn't all about freight. Moving people was also big business. Liverpool was one of the points on the notorious transatlantic slave trade triangle. Ships left the port with goods and headed for Africa, where the cargo was traded for slaves. The same ships then embarked on an often treacherous journey known as 'the middle passage' to America. Men, women and children who survived the crossing were consequently sold to work in plantations.

The slave trade – although not slavery itself – was finally abolished in Britain by an 1807 Act of Parliament, despite vociferous efforts by some Liverpool merchants keen to maintain it for financial rea-sons. Fortunately, there were more people waiting in the wings to fill Liverpool's idle ships, this time willing passengers with an altogether brighter future in mind. It was the age of emigration to destinations such as America, Canada and Australia. Families looking for a new start came from across Britain, Ireland and Europe to Liverpool to take advantage of the numerous available passages and the relatively swift transatlantic journey. Consequently waves of people from many nations arriving or leaving Britain passed through the port. Apart from the wealth generated by ticket prices, there were associated benefits for the city in catering for this transient population. Accordingly businesses such as bars and boarding houses prospered, and as time went on so too did the railway system. In 1852 alone, almost 300,000 people left the Liverpool docks to start new lives in the Americas.

These peoples had an enormous impact on the city and its culture. Peter Grant, a local journalist, historian and specialist in all things Liverpudlian, was enlightening on the issue. 'Scouse,' he explained, 'is an accent, a people and a dish.'

The first two are familiar, but the third is something of an unknown. Originally called Labskause, it turns out to be a mixed casserole dish of mutton and vegetables which had been brought to the city by Norwegian

BY 1872 LIVERPOOL WAS THE NATIONAL FOCUS FOR EMIGRATION.

sailors. 'The dish,' said Peter, 'is a perfect metaphor for Liverpool. You add a bit of this and a bit of that, then put in your spoon and mix. Much like the Scouse accent, which is made up of Scottish, Irish, Welsh, Lancashire and Cheshire accents, and according to where you are in the city it has its own distinct twang.'

From Liverpool we headed east to Rainhill, just 20 minutes down the tracks. Steam trains expert Christian Wolmar waited on the station platform. Although noisy and not that pretty, Rainhill station seemed the most appropriate place for him to talk about what is perhaps the most significant stretch of railway line in the world. As trains thundered past, Christian explained that the first competition between steam locomotives had taken place here in 1829, before train and track were inextricably linked. Indeed, rails had been in existence for years, usually extending between mines or quarries and nearby industrial centres. Loaded wagons were usually pulled by horses. At the time of the contest the notion of an independently powered engine doing the donkey work was still new.

It seems extraordinary now, but the 1829 Rainhill trials were organised to enable the directors of the Liverpool & Manchester Line to decide whether the trains should be powered by locomotives or by stationary steam engines. Five locomotives took part, one of which was powered by a horse walking on a drive belt, and were timed over the same course, with and without carriages. There was a £500 prize for the victor, whether or not a locomotive was eventually chosen. George Stephenson's *Rocket* won hands down, having achieved a top speed of 30 m.p.h., and set a steam locomotive agenda for the Liverpool & Manchester Line, and ultimately the rest of the country. The display was enough to convince any remaining doubters that locomotives were the way forward as far as rail travel was concerned.

A year later the line was opened by the Prime Minister, the Duke of Wellington. But Stephenson's day of triumph was marred by the death, not far from where we stood, of Merseyside MP William Huskisson, who became one of the first victims of the modern railway.

Huskisson accidentally opened a carriage door in front of the oncoming *Rocket*, was knocked off balance and fell beneath its wheels. Although the Conservative MP was rushed by train to the town of Eccles by Stephenson himself, he died there within a few hours. His untimely death gave ammunition to a stalwart band of nay-sayers who opposed the railway on the grounds that it was new, that it threatened

STEPHENSON'S ROCKET WAS THE WINNER OF A STEAM LOCOMOTIVE COMPETITION HELD IN RAINHILL IN 1829 THAT DETERMINED A BRIGHT FUTURE FOR THIS NEW TECHNOLOGY.

long-established ways of life and that there were unknown dangers associated with it that had yet to become apparent. Iron roads were not welcome everywhere they went. But despite Huskisson's demise it was apparent that the age of rail, indeed rail mania, was here to stay.

Eccles was the next destination for us too. Heading out towards Manchester through the sprawling housing estates, we wondered what Eccles had to offer the Victorian traveller and turned to Bradshaw to find: 'The little village is prettily situated on the northern banks of the Irwell and environed by some of the most picturesque rambles.'

The railway changed all that. Within 30 years, Eccles had been swallowed up into the suburbs of Manchester. Even in Bradshaw's day, though, Eccles's claim to fame wasn't so much about being a pretty village. It was about the cakes produced there.

BELOW: **ECCLES CAKE MAKING WAS BIG BUSINESS.**

OVERLEAF: **MILL STACKS LOOMED LARGE BY THE RIVER IRWELL IN MANCHESTER BY 1859.**

Nobody knows for certain when Eccles cakes were created, but they definitely predate the railway. In the seventeenth century Cromwell and his Puritans even banned them, on the grounds that they were too rich and sumptuous. Fortunately for Eccles and the rest of the Puritan-weary population, the ban was lifted during the Restoration. James Birch opened the first shop in the town to sell Eccles cakes on a commercial basis in 1796. There followed some rather ill-natured rivalry – and even today the townsfolk hold that a cake made outside of Eccles cannot truly be called an Eccles cake.

What the railways did was to make it quick and easy to ship the cakes all around the country. It has also been claimed that they were responsible for a change in ingredients. At the time the cakes were sold from station platforms and laced with brandy to help preserve them. But, the story goes, one driver enjoyed a generously laced Eccles cake too many and fell off his footplate, almost causing a crash. From then on, brandy was banned for the railway's Eccles cakes, though it was still used to preserve cakes made for export to America and the West Indies.

Today the cake is as popular as ever. Ian Edmonds is the fourth generation of his family to produce Lancashire Eccles cakes. The secret of their success, he explained, lies in the ingredients. Ian uses only the very best currants money can buy. Called Vostizza A, they come from a Greek farmers' co-op in a town near Corinth – from which we get the word currant. Ian's team carefully wash 10 tonnes each week to quality-control the fruit. The plumped-up currants are then encased by hand in buttery pastry in a factory that produces 150,000 Eccles cakes a day for the domestic and export markets.

From Eccles the train brought us swiftly into Manchester, to discover more about cotton and the railway. It was clear from reading Bradshaw that the fortunes of the two were intertwined. By the 1830s Manchester was well established at the heart of the cotton industry, but the creation of the line to Liverpool and the subsequent lines that followed transformed its fortunes. At its peak in 1853, there were 108 mills in Manchester and it became known as Cottonopolis.

That history is still evident in the city's buildings and streets. Local journalist-cum-tour guide Jonathan Schofield believes the only way to see the city so as to take it all in is to walk. From the Royal Exchange, where the cotton lords met each Tuesday almost 200 years ago, through the Godlee Observatory on Sackvillle Street, named after local mill

ECCLES'S CLAIM TO FAME WASN'T SO MUCH ABOUT BEING A PRETTY VILLAGE. IT WAS ABOUT THE CAKES

owner Francis Godlee, to the iron street kerbs found around the city built to protect the pavements from the overloaded carts, cotton resonates on almost every route around Manchester. It was cotton that turned Manchester into the fastest-growing city of the nineteenth century.

The terrible congestion, squalid living conditions and harsh working conditions led to unrest, with strikes and food riots culminating in the Peterloo massacre, in which 11 people were killed and hundreds injured. Manchester was at the forefront of the movement towards reform that led to the Factory Acts.

Another of Manchester's many claims to fame is that in 1801 George Bradshaw, author of our guide to Victorian Britain, was born here, in fact just outside the city in Pendleton, near Salford. Bradshaw was an engraver and cartographer who completed a detailed record of the canals of Lancashire and Yorkshire in 1830, known as *Bradshaw's Maps of Inland Navigation*.

When the railways arrived he spotted a lucrative gap in the market and in 1839 started publishing one-off, then monthly timetables in a yellow wrapper which later graduated into a round-England and then a Continental guide. Within four years an eight-page pamphlet had grown to 32 pages, drawing together the times and services run by numerous rail companies. Without Bradshaw passengers were dependent on locally produced timetables that rarely extended beyond the often narrow boundaries of the rail company itself.

His name swiftly became a byword for timetables and featured in several Sherlock Holmes stories and in Bram Stoker's *Dracula*, reflecting its hallowed place in society. Phineas Fogg began his adventure in Jules Verne's *Around the World in Eighty Days* with a copy of Bradshaw under his arm.

An active Quaker, Bradshaw was also notable, if less well known, for his charitable works among the poor of Britain's industrial heart-lands. Bradshaw died of cholera in August 1853 during a visit to Norway, where he is buried. But his products continued to flourish, their popularity unabated despite their somewhat complex content. It wasn't until the eve of the Second World War that Bradshaw stopped appearing in print. By this time rail companies were keen to publish timetables of their own.

Whilst much of what Bradshaw marvelled at still exists, today's Manchester is a very different place. The decline of the cotton industry

began with the American Civil War in the 1860s, when supplies faltered. The perils of an industry reliant on raw materials grown a vast distance away became starkly apparent. It was only a matter of time before other producers working with reduced costs, including America, Japan and India, began to challenge Manchester's dominance. The mill owners were also slow to update their antiquated machinery, making them less competitive than ever. No amount of import tariffs could halt the inevitable. The Manchester mills were doomed.

Some mills made way for modern developments. Others have been transformed into flats and hotels. The cause of another great change to the city skyscape was the IRA bombing of the Arndale Centre in 1996, which injured more than 200 people and caused £1 billion of damage. Today the surviving mill buildings are surrounded by steel and glass in a city that looks firmly forward whilst still acknowledging the past.

WHOLE FAMILIES RELIED ON MILLS FOR EMPLOYMENT.

There is no more eloquent memorial to that past than the former terminus of the Liverpool & Manchester Railway, which now houses the Manchester Museum of Science and Industry. It is the oldest passenger railway station in the world.

The next leg of our journey took us on a short detour south-east to Denton to visit what was left of another Victorian success story, again driven by the railways – the hat industry. In Bradshaw's Britain there were 90 hat factories around Denton, and at one point almost 40 per cent of the local population was employed in them. It's claimed that the trilby, perhaps one of its finest creations, was born here.

In Denton we found a tale mirrored up and down the country – one of expansion during the second half of the nineteenth century followed by rapid contraction, leaving a few very specialist high-end producers. The period of growth was often tied in with the arrival of the railways, which allowed companies to move their goods further, faster and more cheaply. The contraction usually came as it became cheaper to produce the goods in alternative markets. In Denton, there was a twist.

Denton's felt hat industry had already had a tough time at the hands of the whims of fashion, but its eventual demise was the result of another major invention in transportation – the motor car. After all, who needs a hat when all you have to do is jump in your car? The result is that the only factory remaining is Failsworth Hats.

At Failsworth's, hats have been produced in much the same way since the company was established in 1903, using virtually original machinery. However, manager Karen Turner highlighted one significant change. Up until the twentieth century, mercury was used to separate rabbit hair from the hide used to make felt hats. Not surprisingly, many of workers in daily contact with rabbit hides suffered from poisoning. Symptoms included erratic behaviour and dementia, and it's this, they say, that gave rise to the phrase 'mad as a hatter'.

From Denton we headed north past Ilkley Moor, and back in time, to catch a steam train on the Embsay & Bolton Abbey Steam Railway just on the edge of the Yorkshire Dales. One of my great discoveries making the series was how many steam trains there are still in existence around the country carrying holidaymakers and even commuters. This railway, part of a branch line that was closed by the Beeching cuts in the 1960s, was reopened in stages as a heritage line from 1981 to 1998, when Bolton Abbey station was reopened.

THE PERILS OF AN INDUSTRY RELIANT ON RAW MATERIALS GROWN A VAST DISTANCE AWAY BECAME STARKLY APPARENT

Stephen Middleton, who met us at the station, is unusual even among those passionate about the railway. He doesn't record their numbers or photograph them. He doesn't even drive them. What he does is buy and restore old carriages which are then used, for example, on the Embsay & Bolton Abbey Steam Railway. His aim is to recreate the magic he felt as a boy, riding on a privileged ticket, thanks to his father's job on the railway, in a first-class carriage. It was a boyhood sensation enjoyed by many and rarely bettered. And it was certainly the best way to travel in the age of steam.

Undoubtedly it sounds romantic today, but steam locomotive travel was dirty and smelly, particularly for third-class passengers in the early days who travelled in coaches that were little more than open-topped wagons lined with benches. As if being open to the elements wasn't enough, there was also the hazard of burning sparks and soot spewing from the locomotive. But the idea that everyone could afford at least one trip a week on the railway was enshrined in law in the 1840s, after which all railway companies had to offer at least one 'open to all' ticket. Quick and cheap, a new phenomenon of day-tripping was created by the railway. Almost overnight, Bolton Abbey became a day-trip sensation.

The Abbey is on the 30,000-acre estate owned by the Dukes of Devonshire since 1755. In 1888 the then Duke realised the potential of turning it into a tourist destination and built a station to accommodate day-trippers who came there to marvel at the unspoilt views. Even Bradshaw was wowed by the Abbey and its stunning location, in his stiff sort of way: 'The Abbey is … most charmingly situated on the banks of the river Wharfe. Indeed the picturesque character of this and surrounding districts in peculiarly striking and impressive.'

The Abbey has retained its magic and the journey by steam makes getting there a fantastic adventure, visitors experiencing it today in much the same way as Bradshaw did all those years ago.

For the next part of our eastward journey to York, we were lucky enough to take to the air, something that George Bradshaw would have loved. In his day the railways were kept safe by railway staff called policemen – although they were not part of any constabulary – who had positions at key points along the lines. There were no signals and the policemen's job was to ensure that there was a 10-minute gap between the trains, holding them up if not. They also walked the lines to check for debris. Now, though, the Network Rail helicopter full of gadgets and

RIGHT: **HERITAGE LINES LIKE THE EMBSAY AND BOLTON ABBEY STEAM RAILWAY HAVE LONG BEEN POPULAR WITH YOUNG AND OLD.**

OVERLEAF: **PICTURESQUE BOLTON ABBEY REMAINS EASILY ACCESSIBLE BY TRAIN.**

gizmos does much of that work, including using infrared cameras that show whether the heating system on the points is working properly. The helicopter regularly surveys the 20,000 miles of Network Rail track, a feat that would have kept thousands of Victorian policemen busy.

However you approach York, it is a beautiful city. Entering it by rail, though, there is the added beauty of the station itself. Designed by architects Thomas Prosser and William Peachey, it was built in 1877 and was the largest station in the world. It's now one of the busiest, with 400 trains passing though it every day, bringing many of the 4 million visitors who come to York each year.

There's plenty to see. Although best known as a medieval city, York started out in AD71 as a settlement beside a huge 50-acre Roman fortress which housed 6,000 soldiers. It was more than just an important military base: for a short time when the Emperor Severus lived there in 209 the entire Roman Empire was ruled from York.

The most enduring legacy of the Romans is the magnificent city walls, including the Multangular Tower. Although many of the walls were there for Bradshaw to see, since then the city has continued to yield up its Roman secrets, and excavations go on today.

From York our route took us towards Hull via Pontefract. We were in search of liquorice, because in Bradshaw's day Pontefract was famous for the black sweet, with plants being farmed in the fields surrounding the town. It's thought that monks had started to grow liquorice there some 600 years ago when they discovered that the area's deep, loamy soil was perfect for the plant's long roots. They used the roots for medicinal purposes, extracting the sap and using it to ease coughs and stomach complaints.

After the Dissolution of the Monasteries in the sixteenth century, local farmers continued to cultivate liquorice and a thriving cottage industry was established. Then, in 1760, Pontefract apothecary George Dunhill made a breakthrough. He added sugar to the recipe and created the liquorice cake sweet.

Before the railways, almost all the liquorice grown was used locally, but the arrival of the trains saw it transported nationwide. More of the surrounding land was turned over to growing it. There's scant trace of it now, though.

Tom Dixon's family grew liquorice for over 200 years, and in their heyday they supplied Boots – it was a chief ingredient for their throat

YORK STATION WITH ITS
BOLD LINES AND GRACEFUL
ROOF WAS AN OBJECT OF
PRIDE FOR ITS STAFF.

sweets. Tom told us that his great-grandfather had even sent liquorice down to Queen Victoria, who was said to adore it. He did so without realising that liquorice brought on high blood pressure, which is what led to her demise.

The death of Pontefract liquorice came much later. It was grown in the fields around Tom's house until the late 1960s, when the last harvests took place. Indeed, Tom is said to have Pontefract's last liquorice bush. Like so many products that boomed for a while with the arrival of the railways, it had become cheaper to import it from elsewhere as travel costs fell across the board. For liquorice, the primary markets became Spain, Italy and Turkey. Curiously, liquorice was known locally as a stick of Spanish – it had originated in Spain.

After the short stop in Pontefract, we were back on the train heading east towards the city and North Sea port of Kingston upon Hull, better

known today as Hull. Bradshaw explains that this was one of the earliest routes used for the popular day-trips which started in 1840 and were known as Monster Excursions.

One of the first Monster Excursions took place in August 1840 when a special Sunday train set off from Leeds to Hull. Organised by the Leeds Institute, it had an incredible 40 carriages transporting 1,250 passengers for the day. Trips like these not only did a huge amount to publicise the idea of railway excursions, but also made Hull a recognised destination. This information might have some locals snorting into their sleeves, but, thanks to Bradshaw, we can glimpse a surprising view of Victorian Hull.

'It presents the eye an interesting spectacle of numerous vessels floating to and from the port of Hull: while that opulent and commercial town in its low situation close to the banks and surrounded by the masts of the shipping in the docks seems to rise like Venice from amidst the sea; the whole comprising a scene which for beauty and grandeur can scarcely be exceeded.'

Believe it or not, Hull was an attractive resort in Victorian times, the sort of place Queen Victoria was happy to visit. In 1854 she stayed in what swiftly changed its name to the Station Hotel, shortly before enhancing it with the prefix 'Royal'. Built in 1851, it was probably the first railway hotel of its kind, literally straddling the platform. It also gets a mention in Bradshaw, along with the zoological gardens, the camera obscura, the music hall, the Crystal Palace and the fireworks held every Monday evening during the season!

Hull's sheltered location on the Humber estuary led to it developing as a prosperous port. Initially the wealth came from whaling, which until the 1840s was subsidised by the government. At much the same time as the subsidy disappeared, the railway line arrived, opening up the opportunity of new markets. The whalers turned to fishing and Hull soon became one of the biggest white fish ports in the world.

The railway was crucial to Hull's growth. There were some 300 miles of railway track transporting fish within the city boundaries, and 20 fish trains left Hull every day for destinations all over the UK, including Manchester's new fish market. Consumption grew from three to 80 tons a week and at a quarter of the price it had been previously.

Hull remained an important white fish port until the 1970s, when the industry collapsed following the Third Cod War. In 1975 Iceland placed a 200-mile exclusion zone around its coastline. Britain refused to recognise the barrier and its trawlers continued to fish in the newly created Icelandic waters. When they were confronted by Icelandic ships the Royal Navy became involved. Although a few shots were fired, it was mostly a war of ramming and stand-offs, peppered with net-cutting incidents.

Almost wholly dependent on fishing, Iceland took its action in the face of diminishing stocks. Britain also realised that fish catches were dipping, but resented the strategic action taken by its small, northerly neighbour. A compromise was eventually reached which permitted a small number of British ships to trawl in the disputed waters while limiting their catch.

The writing was on the wall for the East Coast fishing fleets. In 1977 there were 127 trawlers working out of Hull, but within two years that number had gone down to just six. Today, 97 per cent of our cod is imported and, with the temperature of our coastal waters rising, that's unlikely to change.

If there is an upside to the rising temperature of our coastal waters, it is that other fish like sea bass can tolerate the North Sea. In fact, over the last decade the east Yorkshire coastline has seen a steady increase in the number of sea bass, so we decided our next stop would be Bridlington, 25 miles up the coast, to find the antidote to over-fishing.

Bradshaw describes Bridlington thus: 'This attractive resort lies on the Yorkshire coast, but at that point where the line turns westward from Flamborough Head and then sweeping round to the south forms a capacious bay called Bridlington Bay ... the Esplanade is a spacious level green commanding a beautiful view of the Holderness coast which stretches in a curve as far as the eye can trace.'

The arrival of the railway in 1846 had turned the sleepy fishing village into a popular resort for West Yorkshire's industrial workers and, with much of that Victorian esplanade still intact, it still attracts thousands of holidaymakers every summer.

Fisherman Frank Powell pursues his trade in a way that's about as far away from giant trawl nets and factory ships as you can get. He chooses to fish sustainably, so much so that he doesn't even leave land. He fishes for sea bass from the shore, using a system that relies on the tide, and he only takes a few fish each time. What's more, Frank uses a net that only keeps fish of a certain size, making it a method of fishing which should see stock protected for future generations. Who knows, in years to come maybe the fish in our fish and chips is more likely to be red mullet or sea bass than cod or haddock.

97 PER CENT OF OUR COD IS IMPORTED AND, WITH THE TEMPERATURE OF OUR COASTAL WATERS RISING, THAT'S UNLIKELY TO CHANGE

VICTORIAN VISITORS TO BRIDLINGTON RELISHED THE SIGHT OF SQUALLING WAVES AROUND THE CLIFFS AT FLAMBOROUGH HEAD.

GALES REGULARLY
SMASHED FISHING
BOATS ALL ALONG
THIS COAST, BUT
THE FISHERMEN
FROM FILEY WERE
PARTICULARLY
AT RISK

Winding our way up the coast, our next stop was Bempton, just four miles along the track. Bempton was the closest we could get by rail to the magnificent Flamborough Head, which turned out to be every bit as impressive today as it was in Bradshaw's time, with its 'lofty cliffs of nearly five hundred feet elevation, teeming in the spring and summer months with thousands of birds of every hue and species and exhibiting yawning caverns of stupendous size'.

Meeting Ian Kendall from the Royal Society for the Protection of Birds, Michael discovered that the beautiful, unchanging scenery belies a worrying decline in the North Sea bird population. The change in water temperature over the last 25 years has decimated the sand eel population which is a major food for the birds. The tragedy is that many species of bird are simply starving, leaving them unable to breed and threatening their future.

This coastline also boasts two lighthouses that are worth a mention and a visit. The Chalk Tower is an ancient beacon built around 1674 which lays claim to being England's oldest lighthouse. Then there's a far more recent one designed by architect Samuel Wyatt and built by John Matson in 1806 for the princely sum of £8,000. Wyatt's lighthouse used red glass for the first time, giving the characteristic lighthouse flash of two white flashes followed by one red flash. The red flash was easier to see in thick fog and was quickly adopted in other lighthouses.

Another 15-minute hop up the coast lies Filey, which is described by Bradshaw simply as 'modern'. When the railways arrived in 1846, Filey grew as a quieter alternative destination for visitors wanting to avoid its more lively neighbour, Scarborough.

Tourism wasn't the only industry growing in Filey. Fishing was expanding too, and in 1870 there were 100 vessels manned by around 400 men. But it was a tough and dangerous job on the treacherous coast here, and many lost their lives. Bradshaw makes an oblique reference to the tragedy of fishing here, observing that 'owing to a great number of men being drowned in 1851, the population of women is considerably greater than that of the men'.

It's not clear exactly which disaster he's referring to, or whether it was one or several, but it's not difficult to believe. Gales regularly smashed fishing boats all along this coast, but the fishermen from Filey were particularly at risk. They used and still use boats known as cobles, which are flat bottomed with no keel, making them easy to launch and land at the

FLAMBOROUGH LIGHTHOUSE,
BUILT IN 1806 AND AUTOMATED
SINCE 1996, ACTS AS A BEACON
FOR SHIPS TO BRIDLINGTON.

beach. They also have high bows, which make them better for ploughing directly into the surf. They are very stable for their size, but the men of Filey used them for winter fishing. Whilst boats from neighbouring towns were laid up, the men of Filey were out long-line fishing at a time when gales were most likely.

It was so dangerous that the tradition of knitting jumpers took on a different, darker role. The style and pattern of these not only varied from town to town but also from family to family – to ensure that bodies of people lost at sea could be identified.

In the neighbouring coastal towns fathers and sons worked on different boats to prevent whole families being killed. For the men of Filey, the tradition was for a man to be accompanied by his sons on his boat, this being the best way to pass on the necessary skills. But it meant that the cost to one family following a tragedy was immeasurable. It's claimed by Filey people that, proportionately, no maritime community has lost so many men as their own.

Scarborough, the final stop on our journey, has also had its fair share of fishing boat disasters. But the town's sons had other career options. Scarborough had long been a holiday destination for the rich, who were attracted to the spa and its iron-rich waters. Indeed, their beneficial effects were well known in the seventeenth century, and the town can claim to be England's first seaside resort. Once the railways put the town on the map as a major holiday destination for the masses, the numbers increased dramatically. As Bradshaw writes, 'There are thirty-three miles of coast which may be inspected at low water over a course of the finest sands in England.'

As the cotton mills across the north-west closed for a holiday called 'wakes week', the workers headed to the coast, and especially to Scarborough. Bradshaw describes many attractions in detail: the iron bridge, the twelfth-century castle and hilltop walks complete with panoramic views. But they also flocked to see a skeleton called Gristhorpe Man. On his discovery in July 1834, the remains of this Bronze Age man became a national sensation. It was thought to be the best-preserved example of an oak tree trunk burial – a coffin made from a hollowed-out tree usually reserved for a tribe's elite – and Victorians travelled from far and wide to see him.

Gristhorpe Man is still on display in the town. In 2005 a team of experts arrived to take a closer look and were at first sceptical. He was so

SCARBOROUGH, THE FINAL STOP ON OUR JOURNEY, HAS ALSO HAD ITS FAIR SHARE OF FISHING BOAT DISASTERS

well preserved that they were convinced he was a fake. But after a close examination using the most modern forensic tests they concluded that he was in fact a genuine Bronze Age man who had died in his sixties, possibly from a brain tumour. Tests also revealed that he was likely to have lived locally, on a high-protein diet full of meat, and had kidney stones. Even after 2,000 years, modern methods were able to peel away Gristhorpe Man's secrets.

Before the railways Gristhorpe Man might have recognised some aspects of English life. Afterwards the fundamentals of everyday living changed. In our 10 days' travelling from Liverpool to Scarborough the enormous impact the railways had on almost every aspect of Victorian life became starkly apparent. In a matter of a few years everything changed in a revolution that then proceeded to sweep the world.

GRISTHORPE MAN DATES FROM THE BRONZE AGE AND DIED IN HIS SIXTIES, PROBABLY FROM A BRAIN TUMOUR.

Nursery

COTH

COTHAM

KINGS

Turnpike

Pembroke Ho

Zoological Gardens

Oakfield Ho

County Boundary

THE PA

Conservative Rooms

Walk out on Hill

Horley Plt

Somerset Place

Chilton Rd   Park Gate

Bishops Coll

Boardhumd Rooms

Blind Asyl

Suspension Bridge

O

N

Horley Sq

Brandon Ho

Chapel

Royal York Crescent

St. Aulton Ch.

Foot Path to Clifton

Clifton Hill

Lower Crescent

Constitution

C

Clifton

WELLS

Robert Road

Sea Bank

Wells St

Pembroke Place

OATIN

The Dock Act of 1803 extends the boundaries of the City for certain objects, to town harbour, to include the Docks together with the paths & roads on each side back to the bottom in Wells.

Ship Yard

Sand Rocks   Corporation

Cliff Ho

Scale

JOURNEY

2

THE HOLIDAY LINE

From Swindon to Penzance

Most of us take it for granted that we'll take a holiday at some time. Indeed the number of Britons going abroad each year is now more than 56 million. Before the spread of trains, though, vacations at home or overseas were exclusively the province of the rich. For want of time and money, the majority could not dream of spending a week or even a day away – until the railway system spider-webbed the country and changed everything. And no line was more instrumental in unshackling swathes of the population from their homes and employment for a short spell than a 300-mile stretch nicknamed the Holiday Line.

Initially the man behind this westward-bound railway was the far-sighted engineer Isambard Kingdom Brunel (1806–59), working for the Great Western Railway. His hallmark designs are still apparent today in the shape of Paddington station, the original Bristol Temple Meads station which stands disused next to the current station, and the Box tunnel, as well as all the bridges, viaducts and other tunnels along the line – engineering feats that doubtless concerned him more than fortnights away. The more westerly sections of the line were in fact not finished until after his death, and it wasn't dubbed the Holiday Line until 1908 by GWR spin doctors.

The Holiday Line still runs between Paddington and Penzance. By the time of its completion, bucket-and-spade holidays had become the norm rather than the exception.

However, it wasn't the spread of railways alone that sparked an explosion in the popularity of British seaside resorts. The Victorian era was the age of philanthropy, and crucially employers began to embrace the idea of holidays for the workers, none more so than those at the Great Western Railway.

The GWR was based in Swindon, our first stop along the holiday line. Its enormous works, constructed there in the early 1840s, were described by Bradshaw as being 'one of the most extraordinary products of the railway enterprise of the present age. A colony of engineers and handicraft men.' Soon Swindon, previously a small market town, was wholly reliant on the railway. Although buildings that once held bustling workshops are now empty shells, they are testament to the thriving industry that was once centred here.

When it first opened the GWR works employed 200 men. A decade later the number had risen to 2,000 men, and by the end of the century

THE GENIUS OF ISAMBARD KINGDOM BRUNEL TRANSFORMED TRANSPORT IN ENGLAND'S SOUTH WEST.

some three quarters of Swindon's working population were employed by the railway company. There was no facet of train or track that could not be built or repaired at the vast complex, a fact that inspired pride among the workforce.

Better still from the workers' point of view were the terms and conditions of the jobs. Not only did GWR build an entire village to house its workers, but with it came a school, a church, a hospital, hairdressers, swimming baths, a theatre and even a funeral director's. Then, from 1848, it started to run free trains for employees and their families heading to the West Country every July, a tradition which continued until the 1970s.

ABOVE: **HOLIDAYMAKERS HAD BRUNEL TO THANK FOR PADDINGTON STATION AT THE START OF THEIR JOURNEY WEST.**

OVERLEAF: **GREAT WESTERN RAILWAYS NOT ONLY BUILT TRAINS AND TRACK BUT ALSO SCHOOLS, HOMES AND SHOPS FOR ITS SIZEABLE WORKFORCE.**

These holidays, known simply as 'Trip', were extraordinary feats of organisation. Tens of thousands of people were transported to resorts all over the south-west, the largest recorded trip being organised on the cusp of the First World War. On 9 July 1914, with tensions rising in Europe, 25,616 people headed west on trains that started to leave at four o'clock in the morning.

Trip veterans Ron Glass and Mary Starley, whose fathers both worked for GWR, recall with fondness later trips and the company's cradle-to-grave umbrella of care. 'Virtually the whole town was coming to a standstill for a week,' explains Ron, who was himself a GWR employee.

Dressed in their Sunday best for both travelling and the beach, trippers were assigned trains that left throughout a Friday so as not to disrupt weekend timetables for the rest of the travelling public. The journey itself had a smell, a taste and a rhythm of its own, as packed carriages towed by GWR steam engines painted in Brunswick green sashayed towards the seaside.

Although the train journey was free, families still had to finance their accommodation, which was a challenge when no one prior to the Second World War received holiday pay. The week after trip became known as the dry week, because workers had received no wages and therefore couldn't afford a drink at the pub. Ron remembers his father giving up smoking for a spell each year to pay for the holiday. For Ron, Mary and the thousands of others, their holidays had started at Swindon station, famous in Bradshaw's day for having had the first refreshment rooms in the country. At the time, there were no buffet cars or tea trolleys on trains, so every GWR train stopped at Swindon for a 10-minute break. According to Bradshaw, the rooms were 'abundantly supplied with every article of fare to tempt the best as well as the most delicate appetites and the prices are moderate, considering the extortions to which travellers are occasionally exposed'.

The story Bradshaw didn't know, or at least didn't tell, was that when Brunel was building the Swindon complex he was so short of money that he struck a deal with his contractors. They built the works, houses and the station in return for the rent revenue and a lease on the station refreshments, 'with the obligation that Great Western stop all trains there for ten minutes for the next hundred years and refrain from offering alternative catering'. It was a deal that stayed in place until 1895, when the company finally bought itself out.

THE JOURNEY ITSELF HAD A SMELL, A TASTE AND A RHYTHM OF ITS OWN, AS PACKED CARRIAGES SASHAYED TOWARDS THE SEASIDE

From Swindon, the train heads south-west to Bath, passing through one of Brunel's most spectacular engineering achievements. Brunel knew that the straighter the route, the faster his trains would go, so Box Hill in Wiltshire, five miles east of Bath, posed a particular challenge. Rather than curve round it and lose speed and time, Brunel made the decision to go straight through it. It was to be the longest tunnel in the world.

It took 4,000 men more than four years to carve a path through the limestone rock – also known as Bath stone. Almost 100 men lost their lives as a tunnel length of 1¾ miles was forged by two gangs, one each side of the hill, who successfully met in the middle thanks to Brunel's astonishingly accurate calculations. In building Box Tunnel, Brunel acquired an adversary, one Dr Dionysius Lardner, who claimed that travelling at speed through a tunnel would render breathing impossible. Put simply, everyone using it would die. When the tunnel finally opened, publicity garnered by Dr Lardner meant that many passengers were too frightened to pass through it. Instead, they left the train prior to Box Hill and took a coach for the remaining distance to Bath. Impossible to know what, 170 years on, nervous passengers would have made of the new Gotthard base tunnel currently being built beneath the Alps, which will be more than 35 miles long.

If Swindon is a shadow of the place Bradshaw trumpeted, the Bath he describes is, for the most part, completely recognisable today: 'Spacious streets, groves, and crescents lined with stately stone edifices and intersected by squares and gardens complete a view of the city scarcely surpassed by any other in the kingdom.' Bath's elegant streets, crescents and circuses remain stunning. The most eminent were designed in the eighteenth century by the renowned architect John Wood (1704–54) and his son, also John, whose genius was to create classical, uniform façades in Bath stone that gave terraced town houses the grandeur of stately homes. Intriguingly, behind the facade the houses are very different from one another, as the original owners were able to dictate the individual layout of their home.

The regimentation was a great success and turned Bath into the playground of high society. That was until the arrival of the railways when, for the first time, the middle and lower classes could afford to travel there and sample what the wealthy had been enjoying for centuries – the spas.

People had bathed here since Roman times, believing the waters – absorbed through skin pores – to be a cure for everything from

ALMOST 100 MEN LOST THEIR LIVES AS A TUNNEL LENGTH OF ONE AND THREE-QUARTER MILES WAS FORGED

TWO GANGS FORGING A TUNNEL FROM EACH SIDE OF BOX HILL IN WILTSHIRE MET IN THE MIDDLE THANKS TO BRUNEL'S ACCURATE CALCULATIONS.

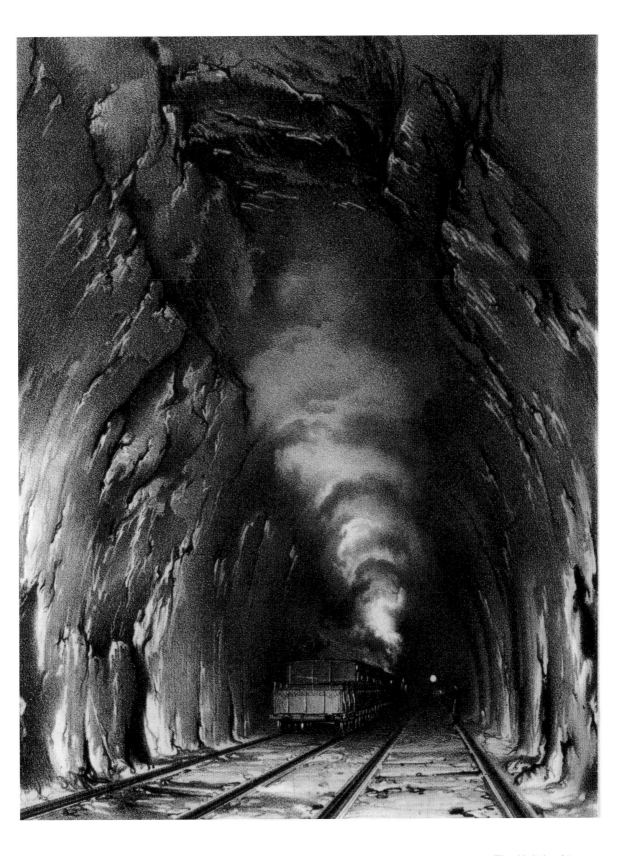

FOR YEARS VISITORS TOOK TO THE SPAS IN BATH, CONVINCED IT WOULD BENEFIT THEIR HEALTH AND WELLBEING.

THROUGHOUT
THE LATE
NINETEENTH
CENTURY,
THE RAILWAY
BROUGHT
ORDINARY
PEOPLE TO THE
SPAS IN THEIR
THOUSANDS

infertility to gout. It turns out they were partially right, but for the wrong reasons. The minerals are not absorbed through the skin, but Dr Roger Rolls, a local GP, historian and author of *The Medical Uses of the Spa*, has studied the water's medicinal properties and points out that it did have some benefits.

The Victorians drank an abundance of cider, port and Madeira, all contaminated by high quantities of lead from the fruit presses. As a result, many of Bath's 'fashionable invalids', as Bradshaw terms them, had ailments arising from lead poisoning. Modern research has shown that immersion in hot water up to the neck increases pressure and makes the kidneys work harder, causing people with raised levels of lead to excrete it more quickly. So the spa water does help with poisoning.

Throughout the late nineteenth century, the railway brought ordinary people to the spas in their thousands, but by the mid-twentieth century the baths fell out of fashion and their doors finally closed in 1978. However, in 2006 – albeit behind schedule and over budget – the Thermae Bath Spa opened. It is a stunning piece of architecture, one that the Woods themselves might have approved. Once again people are flocking to Bath to take the waters, wallowing in a rooftop pool whilst gazing out over the majesty of the city.

From Bath the line heads west, along the valley of the meandering River Avon, to Bristol, where some of Brunel's finest work can be seen, including the Clifton Suspension Bridge and his great steamship *Great Britain*, then the largest ship in the world, and the first large iron-hulled steamship powered by a screw-propeller.

In Bradshaw's day Bristol lay in a different time zone from London. Victorian Britain enjoyed an assortment of times, as clocks were set locally according to the setting sun. London was 10 minutes ahead of Bristol, which was fine until, like Brunel, you were trying to create a timetable for a fast-moving steam train. Brunel's solution was to standardise time across his network, using what he called railway time, and George Bradshaw ably assisted him. When he started putting his timetables together in 1840, Bradshaw also stuck to railway time and ultimately convinced all the other railways to follow suit. Within 10 years the whole country was in a single time zone. It was arguably Bradshaw's most significant contribution to modern society.

REJUVENATED POOLS IN BATH, INCLUDING ONE ON A ROOFTOP, HAVE IGNITED A FRESH DEMAND FOR THE TOWN'S NATURAL SPAS.

IN 1934 BRISTOL TEMPLE MEADS
STATION WAS HECTIC WITH
COMMUTERS AND FREIGHT
AFTER A RECENT EXPANSION.

The grand terminus, Bristol Temple Meads, designed by Brunel and opened in 1840, is today a ghost station. Changes made as Bristol became a major rail junction rendered Brunel's great passenger shed obsolete. From 1999 it was the home of the British and Commonwealth Museum, until that was moved to London. It's not about to be pulled down any time soon, however. The historic nature of the building means that it is still highly prized. What is a shame is that it is now closed, so few people are aware of it and no one steps inside to soak up the grand flavour of the architecture.

Our next stop was at Yatton in Somerset, another reminder of how quickly change occurred with the advent of the railway. In our battered copy of Bradshaw's guide, Yatton barely warrants a mention. Later, in 1868, a new branch line was added, feeding Cheddar into the national network, which put Yatton at the centre of a booming strawberry industry.

The London markets were already catered for by Kent's strawberry growers. But this new branch line, nicknamed the Strawberry Line, meant that for the first time huge quantities of fresh Cheddar Valley strawberries could be whisked around the country, especially to the north. In its heyday, there were 250 growers here producing strawberries which, for those few weeks each year, were picked and transported to market every Friday. Today there are just four growers left, while the Strawberry Line itself fell victim to the Beeching axe in 1964.

LEFT: **BRUNEL'S CAVERNOUS PASSENGER SHED WAS BUILT TO ACCOMMODATE THE ORIGINAL LINE FROM PADDINGTON.**

RIGHT: **BRISTOL'S CLIFTON SUSPENSION BRIDGE WAS ANOTHER OF BRUNEL'S GRAND DESIGNS.**

OVERLEAF: **TOURISM THRIVED AT CHEDDAR GORGE AFTER THE RAILWAY BROUGHT VISITORS BY THE THOUSAND TO THE NEIGHBOURHOOD.**

CLIFTON SUSPENSION BRIDGE

BRISTOL

 Illustrated Booklets from
Development Board, BRISTOL

Sir Richard Beeching, then known as Dr Beeching, was the chairman of the railways at a time when they were considered too costly. The railways had been losing money since the 1950s, and a decade later the government, whose transport minister Ernest Marples was the director of a road construction company, decided enough was enough. Beeching came up with a plan that he believed would save the railways from financial meltdown. It resulted in the loss of 2,128 stations, 5,000 miles of track and 67,000 jobs, with rural Britain the hardest hit. As the expected savings failed to appear on the balance sheet, Dr Beeching's name became a by-word for ill-considered and ineffective cuts. Perhaps the move towards reducing our food miles may yet herald the rebirth of the Somerset strawberry industry.

One local industry that's not in decline is tourism. Before the railway, Cheddar Gorge on the edge of the Mendip Hills was a destination for rich, independent travellers who came to marvel at the deepest gorge in Britain. The trains gave thousands of day-trippers the chance to enjoy it too. They flocked to see what Bradshaw describes as 'a place of some notoriety from the discovery of two caverns in its vicinity, one called the Stalactite and the other the Bone Cave, which now attract a great number of visitors'.

Today half a million people visit each year, but few are as fortunate as my team, who got a personal tour from archaeologist and director of Cheddar Caves and Gorge, Hugh Cornwell. Hugh wanted to reveal a set of caves discovered by an eccentric sea captain and showman called Richard Gough. Gough had turned them into a tourist attraction, the first caves in Britain to be lit with electric light.

As more of the caves were opened to cater for the growing number of visitors, they revealed secrets Bradshaw would have relished. The most important of these was the 1903 discovery of Cheddar Man, the oldest complete skeleton ever found in Britain, dating back some 9,000 years. Examination suggested that as a teenager Cheddar Man had been hit on the head with an axe, but had gone on to live into his twenties. It was odd that he had been buried on his own away from the rest of his tribe. Hugh's theory is that Cheddar Man suffered a brain injury which resulted in antisocial behaviour that doubtless ruffled feathers among fellow tribesmen. When he died, his tribe didn't deal with him in the usual way but buried him instead in the cave, believing it to be a sort of twilight zone that would prevent Cheddar Man's spirit from joining his ancestors in the next world.

From Yatton, the line continues west, past the resorts of Weston-super-Mare, birthplace of John Cleese, and Burnham-on-Sea, before turning inland and heading south. After Bridgwater and Taunton it swings westwards into Devon and then south again towards Exeter and the coast.

The section of route to our next destination, Torquay, is one of the most picturesque rail journeys in existence. Hugging the western side of the Exe estuary and then sliding its way along the coast through Dawlish and Teignmouth, it's a route that's barely changed in the last 170 years. In the words of Bradshaw: 'There is scarcely a mile traversed which does not unfold some peculiar picturesque charm or new feature of its own to make the eye dazzled and drunk with its beauty.'

And the line is not only generous with exceptional vistas but remains an extraordinary feat of engineering. This was one of the most challenging sections of the GWR to construct. In fact, the Exeter Corporation wanted it to stay inland but the redoubtable Brunel insisted it follow the coastal wall, which meant boring five tunnels through the cliffs and building four miles of sea wall to protect the tracks. The result is a magnificent, memorable journey, beneath towering red cliffs, with repeated plunges into darkness as the train goes through one tunnel after another, and all within a few feet of the sea. One signal box was built so close to the waves that the signalmen used to be issued with the oilskins worn by sailors.

The line reached Torquay with its warm microclimate in 1848, and immediately the Great Western Railway started promoting the town as a perfect holiday spot. They even coined the phrase 'The English Riviera' to describe the resort. A few years later, Bradshaw is again comparing Torquay with the south of France, suggesting that 'those English invalids who, in search of a more congenial temperature, hastily enter on a long journey to some foreign county and wilfully encounter all the inconveniences attending a residence there' would do better to 'make themselves acquainted with the bland and beautiful climates which lie within an easy jaunt'.

The English invalids seem to have listened. It wasn't long before they were arriving by the coach-load to relax and enjoy the 19 beaches and coves spread over 22 miles of coastline. On one particular Bank

IN THE WORDS OF BRADSHAW: 'THERE IS SCARCELY A MILE TRAVERSED WHICH DOES NOT UNFOLD SOME PECULIAR PICTURESQUE CHARM'

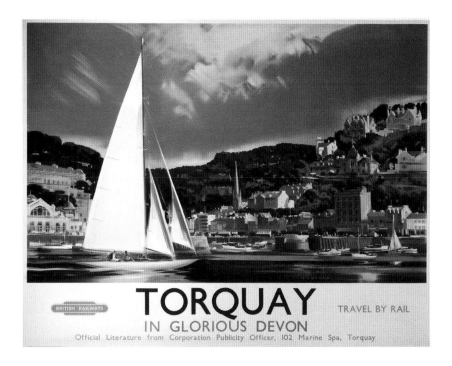

TORQUAY
IN GLORIOUS DEVON
BRITISH RAILWAYS
TRAVEL BY RAIL
Official Literature from Corporation Publicity Officer, 102 Marine Spa, Torquay

Holiday, 20,000 people arrived there by train in a single day. Thanks to the railway, Torquay had become a major resort.

From nearby Paignton it's possible to recreate the train journeys that Bradshaw and Brunel would have recognised. A steam train travels south to Kingswear, first alongside charming beaches among abundant wildlife, then through some of the most idyllic countryside of South Devon by the tranquil River Dart, and all at a sedate 25 miles per hour.

But the railway of Bradshaw's day wasn't only concerned with getting from A to B. It was also about what you did when you got there. Salmon fishing on the Dart became a popular sport for Victorian tourists, and recreational fishermen arriving by train could even buy their fishing permit at the station. In the early 1900s a train laden with salmon and trout from Loch Leven in Scotland would stop at several points along the river to release the exported fish. The railway also encouraged an explosion of commercial salmon fishing, allowing the catch to be swiftly transported inland.

Today salmon stocks have declined in the Dart and there are strict regulations controlling the catch. There are now only three families still licensed to fish for salmon, and all of them have to use the traditional

ABOVE: **SUNNY TORQUAY QUICKLY EARNED ITSELF THE SOUBRIQUET OF 'THE ENGLISH RIVIERA'.**

OVERLEAF: **WITH STUNNING SEA VIEWS AND LUSH COUNTRYSIDE, A TRAIN JOURNEY ALONG THE SOUTH COAST OF DEVON WAS THE STARTING POINT OF A HOLIDAY.**

method called seine-netting. Travelling in an oared seiner, fishermen shoot a weighted net in a semicircle back towards the shore which is then hauled in, often all but empty.

Reading our Bradshaw, it occasionally seemed as though little had changed in 170 years. The book found us hotels, told us what to see, even gave tips for our journey. It was Bradshaw who highlighted that we'd need to take the ferry to cross to Dartmouth because there was no bridge there over the Dart. For nearby Totnes, though, change has certainly come.

Bradshaw was clearly not particularly impressed with Totnes. The book gives the town scant mention. It lists the population as 4,001, suggests one hotel, The Seven Stars, and tells us that, because the town is situated on the River Dart, most people are employed in the fishery. It's a very different place today, with double the population in the Totnes parish alone and a radical outlook.

Totnes is part of a global campaign for sustainability called Transition Towns. It was started there by Rob Hopkins in 2006 as a reaction to climate change and the challenge posed by the age of cheap oil nearing its end. Rob's idea was to treat this as an opportunity rather than a crisis, and in Totnes it seems to be working. One of the key elements is a garden share scheme, which Rob described as being like a dating agency. To reduce the distance food is transported they have a land swap system, putting people who want to grow their own food in touch with people who have spare bits of land they could use.

Totnes also has its own local currency, which can be spent in over 80 shops there. Rob likened Totnes to a leaky bucket, with money coming in and then pouring out again. Of every £1 you spent in a supermarket, 80p was out of Totnes by the next day. But this currency, which you obtain in exchange for cash at one of the local businesses participating in the scheme, can't go anywhere else – it encourages you to spend your money locally and support the town's economy.

Rob's tips for creating your own Transition Town start with finding a few reliable like-minded people to form a steering group. Before your official launch, arrange a few thought-provoking events, so people understand what the issues and aims are. If you can create a groundswell of people fired up on the key issues, you're much more likely to be successful as you move forward. The extraordinary thing is that what started in a small way in Totnes is now being used by thousands of towns, cities and villages around the world.

From Totnes the line skirts the southern edge of Dartmoor and then, after crossing the Tamar at Saltash on Brunel's enormous Royal Albert Bridge (his last great achievement, completed in 1859, the year he died), you are in Cornwall. We carried on west through St Germans, and shortly before St Austell we stopped at a small town called Par, which Bradshaw described as 'a mining town in west Cornwall near the sea with several important mines round it in the granite producing copper, nickel, with clay, and china stone for the Staffordshire potteries'. In fact, Par was an important hub for the huge industry fed by the biggest china clay deposits in the world. For almost 100 years clay used in the Potteries for making porcelain was shipped northwards by sea and canal. In the 1840s the railways took over, and soon it was being ferried on a network of lines that criss-crossed the county.

Most of those lines are long gone now, but one that does still run is used by the clay train that carries 1,140 tons of clay each day to the port of Fowey. Though it rarely takes passengers, we were lucky enough to hitch a ride along a single-track line through stunning Cornish countryside towards to the sea.

Because it's a single track, the trains have a very simple safety system that Bradshaw would have recognised. For the train to go down the track, it has to collect from the signal box a token in the form of a staff, like a heavy relay baton – and there's only one token in circulation for the line, so once you have it you know there's nothing about to come the other way.

The first Cornish clay mines opened in 1746, and by the middle of the eighteenth century 60,000 tons were being extracted each year. Although there are only three mines in operation now, thanks to modern techniques those remaining mines are thriving, extracting 1.5 million tons a year. Today 85 per cent of the total tonnage goes abroad, where it's used for everything from paper whitening to the manufacture of paint, plastics and pharmaceuticals.

Many of the scars left by the closed mines have been disguised with landscaping, but one pit has been radically recycled and is now home to the Eden Project. Its two bio-domes, recreating the rainforest and the Mediterranean, are the largest conservatories in the world. The founders didn't want the project to overwhelm the landscape, so they located them discreetly in the disused pit. Supported by a good train service, it's become one of the country's greenest tourist attractions.

Our next stop was only a few miles further down the line at St Austell, the closest we could get by train to the fishing port of Mevagissey on Cornwall's south coast. Whilst the Mevagissey that Bradshaw visited was on the Holiday Line, it was anything but a popular destination at that time, being 'so filthy that it is a very hot-bed of disease, when the cholera is abroad'.

Mevagissey would certainly have been messy, because it was the centre of the pilchard industry, which in the nineteenth century provided jobs for thousands of locals. It wasn't a glamorous profession.

BELOW: **THE ROYAL ALBERT VIADUCT LINKING DEVON AND CORNWALL WAS COMPLETED BY BRUNEL IN THE YEAR OF HIS DEATH AND CROSSES THE RIVER TAMAR.**

OVERLEAF: **MICHAEL PORTILLO GETS THE FEEL FOR A FISHERMAN'S LIFE.**

Men called huers perched overlooking the sea to spy where the sea-birds were fishing for pilchards. These observers, the origin of the phrase 'hue and cry', then alerted local fishermen, who took off in their boats to bring home as many fish from the vast shoals as they could muster. Often the men would be gone throughout the night, not returning until noon the following day, by which time a crowd would have gathered to meet them. Mevagissey women salted and stored the catch in caskets at processing plants called pilchard palaces. At its peak in 1871, the industry caught, cured and transported 16,000 tons of pilchards. Although the size of the catch diminished, possibly due to over-fishing, there remained sufficient to furnish the market.

In Britain pilchards were mostly sold in tins and were traditionally a cheap, popular food for the masses. However, after the Second World War tinned fish was strongly associated with wartime rationing. As a result, by the 1950s pilchards had become one of the least popular foods in Britain.

In 1997 the industry was in crisis, with fishermen earning as little as 1.5p a kilo. However, the humble Cornish pilchard has since enjoyed something of a renaissance after a local factory owner had a rebranding brainwave. He started marketing his common pilchards as 'Cornish sardines' and, thanks to this new Mediterranean image, sales soared. Fishermen were soon earning around a £1 a kilo, making the enterprise economical once more. There are now 12 boats working out of Mevagissey and neighbouring Newlyn that have pilchards in their sights.

Fortunately, in the interim the narrow alleys and cliff-clinging houses that border the picture-postcard harbour transformed Mevagissey from a down-at-heel fishing village to a hub for tourists. With thousands of visitors passing through its streets and lanes each year, its place on the Holiday Line now seems better deserved.

As a guide Bradshaw's book has its shortcomings. Some places would be easy to bypass thanks to his terse entries. Others are a lot more alluring, especially when his entries hint at something that's mysterious and tantalising. That was certainly the case at Perran Sands, where the very simple description refers to 'the remains of an old church of St Piran, an ancient British edifice which had been covered by the shifting sands for centuries'. The more we delved, the more fascinating the story became.

Perran Sands, on the other side of the peninsula from Megavissey, is an amazing landscape, boasting some of the largest sand-dunes in Britain. As it happens, the sands encase not one but two significant Christian sites. St Piran's Oratory was allegedly built by the saint himself after he landed on Cornish shores. It was here that he apparently healed the sick and even gave life to the dead. And here too he saw molten metal ooze from the Cornish slate that he used as a hearth. He shared this information with local people, and a busy mining industry was founded. The Cornish flag, a white cross on a black background, is said to be inspired by the hearth incident.

In the end the wind-blown sands got the better of the Oratory. It was given up to nature and a new church was built, probably in the tenth century. On the principle that sand would not cross water, a site was chosen with a stream forming a boundary between it and the beach.

This new church became a major draw for pilgrims on their way to Santiago di Compostela in northern Spain, where the bones of the apostle St James are said to be buried. The attraction of the Cornish church was presumably various relics, including the head of St Piran kept in a silver casket. (Apparently it was excavated at the start of the twentieth century, but disappeared almost immediately, into the hands of an unidentified thief.)

Unfortunately, the activities of tin miners underground disrupted the stream and allowed sand to encroach on the church. By the nineteenth century plans to build a third place of worship were well underway. Some but not all the stone from the existing church was taken for the new construction.

Clearly St Piran was an inspiration. But, although he is the patron saint of tin-miners and is generally thought of as one of three national saints closely associated with Cornwall, no one knows for certain who he was. According to legend he came from Ireland, where heathens tied him to a mill-stone before rolling him over a cliff and into a stormy sea. The sea immediately became calm and St Piran floated away, landing on the Cornish coast. He lived in Cornwall, performing miracles, until the age of 206.

The shifting dunes have at times parted to reveal both buildings. However, for their own protection, they have been covered again, the sands only serving to enhance the romance of the site.

FOR A TIME IN THE NINETEENTH CENTURY, CORNWALL'S TIN AND COPPER INDUSTRIES DOMINATED THE WORLD

The railways brought visitors to Cornwall, but they were also incredibly important to local industry. As with the china clay mines, a railway system had developed around the tin and copper mines, with mile after mile of tiny branch lines feeding individual pits. Our next stop, at the town of Redruth, was at its heart

Tin and copper had been extracted here for centuries, but the development of the steam engine put Cornwall on the mining map. Steam-powered pumps enabled miners to dig deeper and faster, producing more ore. The same technology developed the steam locomotive, which meant the metals could be quickly and easily transported around the country. For a time in the nineteenth century, Cornwall's tin and copper industries dominated the world. At the end of the nineteenth and through the twentieth century, however, those mines closed one by one, unable to live with competition from tin mines in Australia and Asia and the copper mines of Chile and America.

The South Crofty mine, near the village of Pool between Redruth and Camborne, had been active for some 400 years. In its heyday it was one of Cornwall's most productive mines, but in 1998, when the value of tin fell to uneconomic levels, Cornwall's last tin mine closed its gates, with little hope for a rebirth in the future.

But it now seems, against all expectations, that there could be a future for South Crofty after all. John Webster, Chief Operations Officer of Western United Mines, is sure that a combination of new technologies and a rise in the price of tin means that we may not have seen the last of Cornish metal mining. Just as the steam technology observed by Bradshaw drove the mining industry forward for the Victorians, new technology is doing the same today. John's team are using modern methods of X-ray analysis to test samples of rock for up to 60 different minerals. It's a hand-held device that can be used

LEFT: **CONDITIONS WERE NOTORIOUSLY GRIM FOR TIN MINERS IN CORNWALL.**

OVERLEAF: **RELICS FROM THE MINING ERA CLING TO THE CORNISH LANDSCAPE.**

in mine shafts as the cores of rock are removed, and it has already revealed South Crofty to be sufficiently rich in metals, including silver, zinc, tin and copper, to make its shafts profitable again. John hopes that within five years they will be extracting 750,000 tonnes of ore annually and, if things go well, the total will ultimately be double that. In South Crofty's heyday annual production was only 10,000 tonnes.

Visiting the mine and seeing the shafts drilled out by hand leaves you in no doubt about how dangerous working there in Bradshaw's day must have been. There were no fans and no ventilation. The average lifespan of a miner was under 40 years, with children working there from as young as eight. While vast fortunes were made for some entrepreneurial Victorians, the flipside of this was that the miners and their families remained desperately poor.

Our journey continued by stunning seascapes and some of Britain's most popular holiday resorts. It was very clear from reading Bradshaw that these had become destinations only since and as a result of the arrival of the railways. St Ives, for example, is synonymous today with its artists' community and holidays, but when the railway came in 1877 it was to a town dependent on fishing.

That industry was so important that an enormous pier and harbour had been built in the eighteenth century to handle the 400 or so fishing boats working out of the port. Whilst St Ives still boasts a working harbour, it's mainly pleasure boats that now head out to sea. Its streets and lanes are packed with tourists who have come here to enjoy the beautiful beaches and turquoise seas. The Great Western Railway was enormously instrumental in that change, even buying Treganna Castle, then the home of the Stephens family, high on the hill overlooking St Ives, and turning it into a luxury hotel to promote tourism and rail travel.

For the last leg of our journey, we headed to Penzance – as far west as it is possible to travel by train – completing a journey from Swindon that would have taken two days by horse and coach. The railway cut that time down to about six hours, and changed the people and the towns and villages along the route for ever. Even the tiny remote village of Penzance, at the very end of the Holiday Line, was soon turning its back on its traditional vegetable-growing businesses as it attracted holidaymakers in droves. Today 5 million tourists spend £1.5 billion in Cornwall to ensure its economic survival, in a success story that began 170 years ago with the birth of the modern railway.

THE AVERAGE LIFESPAN OF A MINER WAS UNDER 40 YEARS, WITH CHILDREN WORKING THERE FROM AS YOUNG AS EIGHT

BY 1930 THE VEGETABLE GROWING BUSINESS IN PENZANCE WAS SECOND STRING TO THE TOURISM INDUSTRY, WHICH BEGAN WITH THE ARRIVAL OF THE TRAIN.

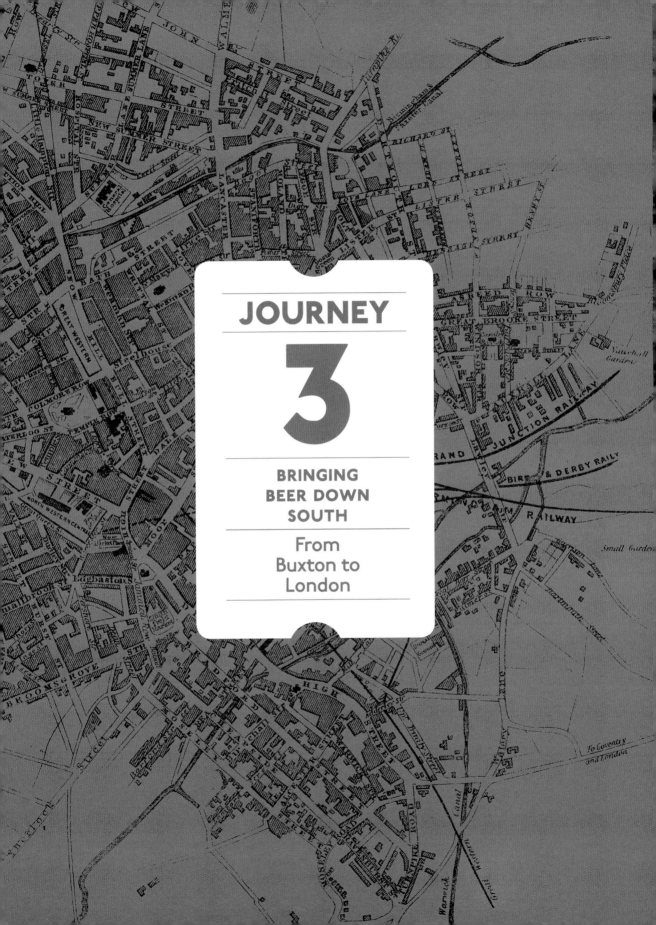

JOURNEY

3

BRINGING BEER DOWN SOUTH

From Buxton to London

These days, most of our freight is transported around the country by road, but in the nineteenth century it was the new railways that hauled goods most cheaply and swiftly, revolutionising industry in the process. Our next journey started in the open spaces of Derbyshire's Peak District on one of the earliest railway routes in England, built to transport freight from north to south. This gave towns at the heart of the Industrial Revolution an artery through which to whisk their goods into the nation's capital. It created booms in the towns through which it passed, and we wanted to retrace that route to see the impact the railways had on these towns and the people living and working in them.

Our first stop was Buxton. Just like Bath, it was founded by the Romans as a spa settlement and in the eighteenth century was an upmarket resort, to which the rich travelled from all over Britain to sample the waters. Even Buxton's architecture mimics its southern sister, with a crescent that Bradshaw describes as 'the principal building of Buxton ... erected by the late Duke of Devonshire and has three storeys and extends for 257 feet'. Built in the 1780s, The Crescent in Buxton was a direct copy of Bath's Royal Crescent, designed by architect John Wood the Younger.

For the next 40 years the Duke of Devonshire led the building of new attractions, including the Opera House, the Pavilion Gardens and the Palace Hotel, all funded by the citizens of Buxton themselves. His vision paid off, never more so than after the arrival of the train in 1863, bringing thousands of paying customers. Buxton flourished as a resort, and the efforts of the incumbent Duke are still reaping rewards. Even though spas have fallen from grace, more than 100 years later these Victorian attractions are still drawing the crowds all year round.

One of Buxton's most magnificent buildings is the Duke of Devonshire's extraordinary stable block which today houses a university campus. According to Bradshaw, it was built at a cost of £120,000, which equates to about £5 million in today's money.

The building, unlike any other stables in the world, is dramatically capped by a huge dome. With a span of 145 feet this dome is larger than those of St Paul's Cathedral and the Pantheon and St Peter's Basilica in Rome. Today, thanks to modern technology, builders can mimic a dome like this or even much larger with little effort, but for its time it was simply breathtaking. It weighs a hefty 560 tonnes and cuts a dramatic

RIGHT: **AN EIGHTEENTH CENTURY OCTAGONAL STABLE BLOCK ROOF WAS REPLACED BY THE WORLD'S LARGEST FREESTANDING DOME AFTER THE BUILDING WAS CONVERTED TO A HOSPITAL IN THE NINETEENTH CENTURY.**

OVERLEAF: **DESIGNERS TOOK HEED OF THE 1879 TAY BRIDGE TRAGEDY, WHICH OCCURRED BECAUSE OF A FLAW WITH THE RIVETS, AND MODIFIED BLUEPRINTS OF THE DOME.**

shape in the Buxton skyline. The dome was finally completed in 1881, over 100 years after the rest of the building, and strangely it probably owes its survival to a distant train crash.

On Sunday, 28 December 1879, the Tay Bridge between Dundee and Wormit was being lashed by a violent storm. The bridge, designed by Sir Thomas Boucher, had opened only the previous summer and was the longest in the world. It also had unusually steep gradients.

No one knows just what happened that night, only that the bridge collapsed as a train crossed at its highest point. The alarm was raised by a signalman, who had waited in vain on the far side of the bridge for the passing of the train. When it failed to appear he went out to investigate, having to crawl on all fours at times to keep his balance in the high winds, and discovered the awful truth. Although there was a search of the Tay that night by steamers, not one of the 72 passengers or three crew was found alive. Indeed, many of the dead were lost to the river waters for ever. Among the victims was Boucher's son-in-law.

When engineers examined the wreckage, they discovered that it was insufficiently braced for high winter winds like those on the night of the disaster. Looking more closely, investigators realised that essential rivets had not been lined up properly with the receiving holes, with the result that rivets sheared off in the high winds and the bridge collapsed.

This shock revelation led to work on similar constructions being halted immediately. These included the Forth Bridge, also designed by Boucher, and the dome on the Duke's stables, designed by architect Robert Rippon Duke. Although the dome was designed to very tight tolerances, prior to the accident a degree of inaccuracy was regarded as acceptable. Where the rivets and holes didn't align, the practice of the time was to force them, which the Victorians called 'drifting' them in. Sometimes the rivets were even heated red hot in order to get them to fit, causing them to lose their shape and strength. Rippon Duke was so worried that he had all the dome's rivets removed and the holes redrilled to align properly, with the result that it stands as strong and proud today as it did when it was finished 130-odd years ago. It was a lesson quickly learnt and one that changed the way the Victorians built, helping them achieve many more incredible feats of engineering that we would pass as our journeys continued.

The lesson was further underlined, as if it were necessary, by the poet William McGonagall (1825–1902), widely regarded as the worst verse-

NO ONE KNOWS JUST WHAT HAPPENED THAT NIGHT, ONLY THAT THE BRIDGE COLLAPSED AS A TRAIN CROSSED AT ITS HIGHEST POINT

writer in British history. His poem about the Tay Bridge catastrophe became his most famous, and it ends like this:

I must now conclude my lay
By telling the world fearlessly without the least dismay,
That your central girders would not have given way,
At least many sensible men do say,
Had they been supported on each side with buttresses,
At least many sensible men confesses,
For the stronger we our houses do build,
The less chance we have of being killed.

Our next destination was Dark Peat in the heart of the Peak District National Park. In Bradshaw's day we would have been able to enjoy the natural beauty through the window of our train. 'The tourists will seldom see such glorious landscape from the window of a railway carriage,' the guidebook says. 'Whilst at one moment the bold hills rise up before us, behind us and on either side, the next a winding valley shows us a charming picture stretching away for miles.'

Although many of the lines that brought Victorian visitors into the National Park have long since gone, more than 10 million people still visit it each year. Britain's first National Park, created in 1951, is a major tourist attraction, reaching into five counties: Derbyshire, Cheshire, Staffordshire, Yorkshire and Greater Manchester.

Park Ranger Chris Dean has become something of an expert on the unforeseen cost of the railways which still haunts some of its most beautiful stretches today. Acid rain from coal-fired industries, including the railways, has caused immense damage to the soil. So much so that the vegetation can't grow back. Where the soil lies bare, the peat – which is a natural store for carbon dioxide from decaying leaf matter – is exposed to the elements and is gradually eroded. As this happens, CO_2 is released into the atmosphere, adding to global warming.

Chris is heading up a team of people dealing with this unfortunate legacy from the Industrial Revolution. They are trying to save the bog and reduce the CO_2 emissions by replanting 35 square kilometres of impaired landscape with vegetation that probably grew there in the first place. It is an enormous job. After treating the soil to reduce its acidity, they plan to plant half a million plants. The first phase, due to

BATHING POOL, NEW BATH HOTEL, MATLOCK BATH. No 6463.

be completed by 2015, should protect the peat from erosion and even encourage more to be produced.

From the peaks we headed to Matlock Bath. Like Buxton, Matlock Bath had long attracted visitors to its thermal springs, and indeed our hotel, which is mentioned in Bradshaw, once boasted its own spa in the basement. When the railways arrived at nearby Ambergate Station in 1840, the town chose a very different route to ensure its survival. No opera house or extensive stables here. Despite being 90 miles from the coast, Matlock Bath decided to model itself along the lines of the big seaside resorts like Blackpool. Funfairs and fish and chip shops opened, along with the town's own annual illuminations, and they're still there today, alongside a more genteel café culture, attracting hundreds of thousands of visitors each year.

For Bradshaw, Matlock Bath conjured up something seemingly rather more international than Blackpool. Our guide calls it 'unquestionably the sweetest and most charming of the Derbyshire spas. It is at the bottom

ABOVE: **THE NEW BATH HOTEL IN MATLOCK BATH BOASTS A HEATED SWIMMING POOL FED BY NATURAL THERMAL SPRINGS, AND HAS BEEN A POPULAR STOP WITH TOURISTS SINCE THE START OF THE NINETEENTH CENTURY.**

OVERLEAF: **SMEDLEY SALESMEN STAND BY TO SELL KNITWEAR ACROSS THE BRITISH ISLES ON BEHALF OF A FIRM THAT CONTINUES TO ENDURE.**

of Matlock dale, a narrow defile, the rocky limestone sides of which are piled up in the manner of the undercliff in the Isle of Wight but covered with a profusion of pine, fir, yew, box and other hardy trees. The scenes through Matlock Bath are exquisitely beautiful and may be compared to a Switzerland in a nut shell.' Although the Swiss nut shell reference now seems odd, it was a well-used travel term in Victorian times, designed to attract tourists.

Our next stop was just nearby, at the sleepy station of Cromford. Today the two trains an hour which stop there belie its past, because in Bradshaw's day Cromford was at the heart of the Industrial Revolution. Bradshaw says simply, 'Here Arkwright built his first mill in 1771.' As Michael put it, 'Never was so much important history crammed into such a small half sentence as that.'

The cotton industry revolved around a network of cottage industries, with people spinning and weaving in their own houses. Entrepreneurial inventor Richard Arkwright (1732–92) brought them all together under one roof in a factory, where they used a mechanical water frame powered by the River Derwent. It was a brand new system, soon to be copied across Britain, and then the world.

Arkwright was born into a poor family but was taught to read and write by a cousin. He didn't turn his attention to the cotton industry until his once thriving wig-making business suffered when hairpieces went out of fashion. Although he is credited with the design of the water frame it was in reality a joint enterprise. In fact, many of his attempts to patent his 'inventions' were turned down in the courts following opposition from jealous rivals and aggrieved fellow inventors. His one undisputed skill was in organising industry, and his enterprises spread across the Midlands, northern England and Scotland. When he died he was a rich man. Arkwright's factory is now a museum, but nearby is another factory, opened 13 years later, which is now the oldest factory still working in the world. It was set up in 1784 by Peter Nightingale, a relative of Crimean nurse Florence Nightingale. He had helped finance Arkwright but decided on a new venture. His business partner was a man called John Smedley, whose family has been producing knitwear here ever since.

Today Smedley knitwear is exported to over 30 countries across the world. Smedley's claim to fame is that the long underpants called long johns were invented here, named after the man who started this factory more than 200 years ago.

FOR BRADSHAW, MATLOCK BATH CONJURED UP SOMETHING SEEMINGLY RATHER MORE INTERNATIONAL THAN BLACKPOOL

At the time the only transport available to take produce from the factories to buyers was horse and cart. The Cromford Canal was completed at extraordinary expense in 1794, but its limitations frustrated burgeoning trade. As early as 1825 Parliament agreed the construction of a wagon way entirely for freight between Cromford and Whalley Bridge – four years before Stephenson's Rocket was up and running. The rail track was completed in 1831, but it was a decade before locomotives were used, and it was another 14 years before passengers could travel on the line, which ultimately closed in 1967.

Fifteen miles further down the line we arrived in Derby, to stay in a hotel recommended by Bradshaw. In fact he didn't just recommend it, he raved about it. Normally, he does little more than list where to stay, but Derby's Midland Hotel gets a whole paragraph. 'It's gratifying to be able to refer to an establishment like this which deservedly enjoys the highest reputation. It possesses all the comforts of a home and there is no lack of spirit necessary to provide to the fullest extent everything which can recommend it to its patron. It is conducted in the most able manner by Mrs Chatfield and may claim to rank amongst the first Hotels in England. If further commendation were needed, we may add that the utmost politeness and economy may be anticipated.'

Opened in 1841, the Midland Hotel was the second railway hotel in England, and the first outside London. It was reserved exclusively for first-class passengers, and there was a tunnel linking it to the station so that luggage could be transferred directly to a traveller's room. Unfortunately you now have to carry your own bags, but today its doors are open no matter which class you travelled in.

Derby, like many places across Britain, was transformed into an industrial centre by the railways. They brought huge wealth and investment to the town. It was a time when great fortunes were made and accordingly beckoned in a golden age of philanthropy. In Derby, one notable act of benevolence was performed by the Strutt family, who gave the town a park. The Strutts had made their fortune in the cotton and silk trade and, in Bradshaw's words, created 'the new Arboretum of 16 acres laid out in 1840 by Loudon, given to the town by Joseph Strutt Esq., – a noble gift estimated at £10,000'.

As Arboricultural Consultant Jonathan Oakes explained to us, this arboretum lays claim to being the first purpose-built public park in England. Up until then, parks had been privately owned by the nobility,

but this was gifted to the council and run for the public. At first entry was free two days a week, and from 1882 this was extended so that there were no charges on any day. For the first time the working classes could enjoy these spaces, previously the province of the rich, and it became the model for public parks around the country.

As our journey continued through England's industrial heartland, we headed south towards the home of brewing, Burton-on-Trent. Its entry in Bradshaw states, 'Bass, Allsopp and Worthington are the chief ale kings here and acres covered with barrels and casks may be seen. Vast quantities of pale ale are exported to tropical climates and drunk by thirsty souls at home as a tonic.'

Before the railways arrived there were only 10 breweries in Burton, but that number quickly tripled. That's when 25 ale trains left Burton every day for destinations all over Britain. The railways were seen as so

PREVIOUS PAGE: **A LOCOMOTIVE RUNNING THROUGH A BURTON BREWERY YARD TO BE LOADED BY BOWLER-HATTED WORKERS.**

BELOW: **MILES OF TRACK WAS LAID INSIDE BREWERY YARDS TO BRING BARRELS FROM THE FACTORY TO THE NEAREST TRAIN STATION.**

important to the industry that brewers started building their own tracks to connect with the main lines run by the railway companies.

Arriving in the town today, the first thing you see is that the barrels and casks have been replaced by enormous silver steel vats stretching into the horizon. It is still clearly a town dedicated to producing beer. Geoff Mumford and Bruce Wilkinson, who co-own the largest independent brewery in town, revealed to us why Burton became synonymous with great beer.

In Bradshaw's day Burton produced one in every four pints of beer drunk in England. This was just the start, though. By 1890 there were over 30 breweries exploiting the local climate, which was perfect for winter fermentation. According to Bradshaw, the other reason the area was so successful at brewing beer was the local water. Bruce concurred, explaining that the hardness of the water is essential to giving Burton beer its taste and its colour. Hard water makes it crisper, cleaner and clearer, making the perfect ale.

The purity of the water also meant that Burton beer could be transported all over the world, starting its journey from the breweries on what, according to Geoff and Bruce, was the biggest private rail network in the country.

There has, not surprisingly, been an environmental cost associated with Burton's beer production: centuries of intense brewing have scarred the landscape. Action to remedy this is in hand with the creation of the new National Forest, a colossal project spreading forestry into parts of Derbyshire, Leicestershire and Staffordshire. Not only are the scars of Buxton being masked, but also those of some defunct coal mines. Millions of trees are being planted which will eventually cover 200 square miles, with tree coverage already three times bigger than it was in 1991. As on Dark Peat, the damage done by our massive industrial expansion is slowly being put right.

Our journey took us next through Walsall and Birmingham, and down to Bournville, a place synonymous with chocolate. When the railway opened in 1874 the station was called Stirchley Street, and five years later the Cadbury family opened their factory there. They needed the railway to transport cocoa and sugar to the factory from the ports of London and Southampton, and to transport manufactured chocolate bars out. They also needed the canals to bring the milk in. Stirchley Street offered both. Before long three trains a day were leaving the factory, each pulling

BEFORE THE RAILWAYS ARRIVED THERE WERE ONLY 10 BREWERIES IN BURTON, BUT THAT NUMBER QUICKLY TRIPLED

60 cars full of chocolate. The Cadburys built six miles of their own internal railway and even ran company engines to take the chocolate to the main line.

As the business grew, brothers George and Richard Cadbury ploughed their profits back into the newly named village of Bournville. Like the best philanthropists of the time, they built new houses for their workers and designed a model community spread over about 1,000 acres. As Quakers, the brothers saw alcohol as the cause of the working class's social problems, so the amenities they laid on did not include pubs. Their argument was that if they provided good living conditions, job security and green spaces to exercise, the workers and their families would build a happy, healthy community. With Bourneville now acknowledged as one of the best places to live in Britain, that idea seems to be as valid today as it did over 100 years ago.

PREVIOUS PAGE: **BROTHERS GEORGE AND RICHARD CADBURY CAME TO BOURNVILLE IN 1879 AND BUILT NOT ONLY A FACTORY BUT A RICH COMMUNITY TOO, IN KEEPING WITH THEIR QUAKER PRINCIPLES.**

BELOW: **LOCOMOTIVES LIKE THIS ONE HAULED CHOCOLATE BARS AFTER THEY WERE MADE AT THE END OF THE NINETEENTH CENTURY.**

Our next stop was Coventry, which is now a very different city from the one Bradshaw visited. Its entry in his book runs to a highly respectable 74 lines, all extolling the city's virtues. 'The fine steeples of St Michael and the Trinity are the first to strike one in this old city which is the seat of the ribbon trade … many old-fashioned gable houses are to be found in the back streets … handsome buildings with noble halls.' Bradshaw's Coventry was essentially a rich medieval city. Built in the fourteenth century, it was once the fourth wealthiest city in England. But one night in 1940, when the Luftwaffe seemed poised to win the battle of the skies in the Second World War, it was all but wiped off the map.

Resident Judith Durant remembers that night well. Judith was 10 years old at the time and explained that, although it began as a normal night, the air-raid siren started just as they were getting ready for bed. She and her family hid in the air-raid shelter in their garden at the start of what turned out to be one of the worst bombing raids on Britain of the war. The operation called Moonlight Sonata saw 600 planes carpet-bomb Coventry for six hours. Five hundred people died as the city was blown to smithereens – targeted because of its great number of munitions and aircraft parts factories. Judith remembers being able to pick out the sounds of the German planes and the whistling of the bombs as they fell; the acrid taste of the dust, so thick you could chew it; enormous explosion after explosion. Judith's memories of that horrendous night will be with her for the rest of her life.

Coventry today is very different from the medieval city that was obliterated that night but, to Judith, every bit as beautiful. One building that encapsulates that rebirth is St Michael's Cathedral. Built to incorporate the ruins of the fourteenth-century cathedral, which apart from its spire was destroyed in the Blitz, it's a very clever piece of sixties architecture by Sir Basil Spence which gives reference and reverence to what was there before but looks forward as well as back.

The surprise about Coventry, though, is that despite the pummelling it received during the Blitz, parts of the medieval city survived. As you wander the streets, there are numerous hints of the Coventry Bradshaw must have seen, and it is certainly somewhere that should still be on the visitors' trail.

We now headed 60 miles south to overnight in Aylesbury, in Buckinghamshire, at the beautiful Hartwell House. It was here that Louis XVIII lived for six years with his family and 100 courtiers during

THE OPERATION CALLED MOONLIGHT SONATA SAW 600 PLANES CARPET-BOMB COVENTRY FOR SIX HOURS. FIVE HUNDRED PEOPLE DIED

his exile from France after the Revolution. Like many stately homes, Hartwell House is mentioned in Bradshaw, which provided the necessary information for Victorian travellers to arrange their own visit with the owners. These days the arrangements are rather easier to make. Like many other stately homes, it's now a hotel.

It's impossible to visit Aylesbury without seeking out its duck. In the eighteenth century Aylesbury duck was a delicacy for the rich. But the arrival of the railways in the 1860s changed that. According to the town's entry in Bradshaw it wasn't long before 'as many as three quarters of a million ducks [were being] sent to London from this part'.

A century ago 'duckers', the area's distinctive white ducks with flesh-coloured beaks, could be found all over the Vale of Aylesbury, but today there is only one farm in the county producing them. Richard Waller's family have been farming Aylesbury ducks since 1775, but it's altogether a much tougher business today.

Until recently, the majority of his ducks were sold directly into London's market at Smithfield – and were transported there by train. Now, owing to new EU regulations, Richard's ducks have again become a speciality exclusive to the area, and around 3,000 of them are sold each year to a local pub, The King's Head, in the village of Ivinghoe. Co-owner George De Maison cooks duck to a recipe perfected over a period of 50 years. For George, the key is using a range of fresh herbs and fruit from their garden, like bay leaves, sage and apples, to lock in and complement the duck's delicate taste.

Twenty-five miles further south, Watford gets a simple mention as 'a busy thriving and populous town consisting of only one street with minor ones diverging from it'. The reason we wanted to stop there wasn't to investigate how much it had grown and changed, which of course it has, but to highlight its role at a particular point in British history.

As early as 1938 the British government had formulated an evacuation plan that would swing into action in the event of war. In fact, the majority of children and mothers with babies from inner-city areas began the evacuation procedure before the declaration of hostilities. In September 1939, in just one week, 3,000 trains were used to evacuate 1.5 million children as part of Operation Pied Piper. By the end of the war, more than 3.5 million children had been relocated.

To reduce the pressure on overburdened stations in London, towns such as Watford were used as departure points. School-aged children

IN SEPTEMBER 1939, IN JUST ONE WEEK, 3,000 TRAINS WERE USED TO EVACUATE 1.5 MILLION CHILDREN AS PART OF OPERATION PIED PIPER

were unaccompanied, except for siblings, and had no idea where they were going to live. For some of the younger children it was an exciting day, as they were herded aboard the packed trains heading out to the country, though none of them had any idea of just how long they'd be away. Some managed only a few weeks, others stayed away from their home for years.

The success of the evacuation often depended on the kindness of the host families. Some of the pairings were disastrous. Country families sometimes complained of lice-ridden, ill-mannered children being foisted on them. Meanwhile some city children felt they were treated like slaves. But for others there was kindness and empathy – and a care-free childhood that would otherwise not have been available to them.

CHILDREN WEARING NAME TAGS AROUND THEIR NECKS ARRIVE IN WALES FROM BIRMINGHAM ON ONE OF MANY TRAINS USED IN OPERATION PIED PIPER, DESIGNED TO SAFEGUARD INNER CITY CHILDREN AND MOTHERS WITH BABIES BY MOVING THEM TO THE COUNTRYSIDE BEFORE THE OUTBREAK OF THE SECOND WORLD WAR.

As Britain became a safer place, children went back to their homes, often meeting a father they didn't remember and a mother they might have seen occasionally but whose wartime experience was completely different from their own. It's impossible to say how many lives were saved by the railways transporting children to safety, but it must have been thousands.

The last stage of the journey took us into London's St Pancras station, gateway to what in Bradshaw's time was the most powerful city in the world, at the heart of an ever-expanding empire. St Pancras is described by Bradshaw as 'the vast and magnificent terminus of the Midland Company eclipsing every other, having a roof 240 feet in span and 150 feet high and faced by a splendid hotel'.

Such was the rivalry between the different railway companies that when St Pancras was built in 1868, with its spires and mock-Gothic style, it was designed entirely to overshadow its neighbour King's Cross, the terminus for the Great Northern Railway, which had been built 16 years earlier. This southern terminus for the Midland main line was not only bigger and bolder than King's Cross, it was the largest enclosed space in the world. Like many London termini, it was also designed around what the railway was transporting, which was beer from Burton. The station was built on 800 columns, each spaced so that barrels could be stored underneath.

Looking at St Pancras today in all its restored glory and with its shiny glass extension stretching the quarter-mile length of a Eurostar train, it is difficult to believe that once, back in the 1960s, this magnificent station was scheduled for demolition. Thanks to a campaign led by the poet John Betjeman it was saved – just ten days before the wrecking balls were due to begin their work – and the station and hotel were both made listed buildings.

The redevelopment of the station cost £800 million, and now, after 75 years of neglect, the hotel is undergoing its own £170 million facelift. Royden Stock, responsible for looking after the hotel before work started, became something of an expert on the building.

Royden revealed to us how the drawings for the hotel had been pro-duced by renowned architect George Gilbert Scott in just three weeks. His design won a competition that attracted 11 distinguished entrants – although his was by far the most expensive. Like all railway compa-nies, the Midland Railway wanted to show off by building the most

LEFT: **BY 1867 THE FOUNDATIONS OF ST PANCRAS RAILWAY STATION INCLUDED STORAGE SPACE FOR COUNTLESS THOUSANDS OF BEER BARRELS FROM BURTON.**

OVERLEAF: **IN A REVAMPED ST PANCRAS MICHAEL PORTILLO IS PICTURED WITH A BRONZE SCULPTURE OF POET SIR JOHN BETJEMAN, WHO FOUGHT TWENTIETH-CENTURY PROPOSALS TO PULL DOWN THE STATION.**

impressive railway hotel in the country, to be called the Midland Grand. Scott's extravagant Gothic style seemed perfect.

Today, as the restoration work continues, more of the original building is uncovered from behind false walls and ceilings. The most impressive feature of all, though, is a stunning cantilevered staircase that seems to float in mid-air as it leads up towards a ceiling painted with stars.

When it opened in 1873, the hotel catered for the wealthiest travellers. Its rooms were amongst the most expensive in London, costing 14 shillings a night. Time caught up, though, and the lack of en suite bathrooms eventually drove guests to other, newer hotels. Hopefully, when its 245 rooms open again for business in 2011, the guests will return.

People often wonder why St Pancras, King's Cross and Euston were all built so close to one another. The reason is that in 1846 Parliament had decreed that all new stations in London had to be built on the edge of the city. A box was drawn around the city's heart, protecting it from railway development. It reflected the views of a powerful lobby that wanted to protect the capital's historic buildings from 'railway vandalism'. It was time, that lobby decided, to stop the railway marching forward at the expense of everything in its path. The result gave the railway companies the perfect opportunity to build ever grander stations. It also led to a revolutionary new transport system to fill in the gaps, called the London Underground.

The world's first underground line, the Metropolitan, was built in 1863 and ran between Paddington and Farringdon, bringing passengers from the railway termini and commuters into the city. Two special trains were run each day for the poorest workers, on which tickets cost only a third of the normal fare. When the line was built, the carriages were pulled by steam trains, so the tunnels had to have openings allowing steam to escape.

For the final part of our journey, we left the trains behind and followed in Bradshaw's footsteps, taking his walking tour of the capital that starts with St Paul's Cathedral, one of London's most impressive buildings and considered by many to be Sir Christopher Wren's masterpiece.

The original cathedral was destroyed in the Great Fire of London in 1666. It fell to Christopher Wren, Commissioner for Rebuilding the City of London, to design and build a replacement, one of 52 churches he was charged with creating. It took Wren 10 years and a number of attempts to come up with the successful design, based on

WREN STARTED WORKING ON ST PAUL'S WHEN HE WAS IN HIS THIRTIES AND WAS 78 BY THE TIME IT WAS FINISHED

the Latin cross and incorporating a large dome. Wren started working on St Paul's when he was in his thirties and was 78 by the time it was finished, but there is no denying it was certainly well worth the wait. As Bradshaw states, 'It's extreme beauty and colossal proportions are worthy of the highest admiration.' Even today, St Paul's Cathedral has a dramatic and romantic impact on the city skyline.

'The most conspicuous object is the river,' says Bradshaw, 'winding its way like a huge artery, beautiful and picturesque bridges spanning the stream.' He recommends standing in the middle of Waterloo Bridge, from where, today as then, you can see St Paul's Cathedral, Somerset House and the Houses of Parliament. Despite 150 years of development, those three buildings still rate amongst the finest the city has to offer.

IN 1862 SELECTED DIGNITARIES TRIALLED THE METROPOLITAN LINE, TRAVELLING AT CLOSE QUARTERS ABOARD SMITH & KNIGHT WAGONS INTO TUNNELS THAT WOULD QUICKLY FILL WITH STEAM AND SOOT.

MARY
BU

Coli

WORKINGTON

Harrington

Moresby

Parton

Saltu
Bank

WHITEHAVEN

Hensingham

Sandwich

Lighthouse

Fleswick

St BEES

Uppertown

Beckerm

St Bridge

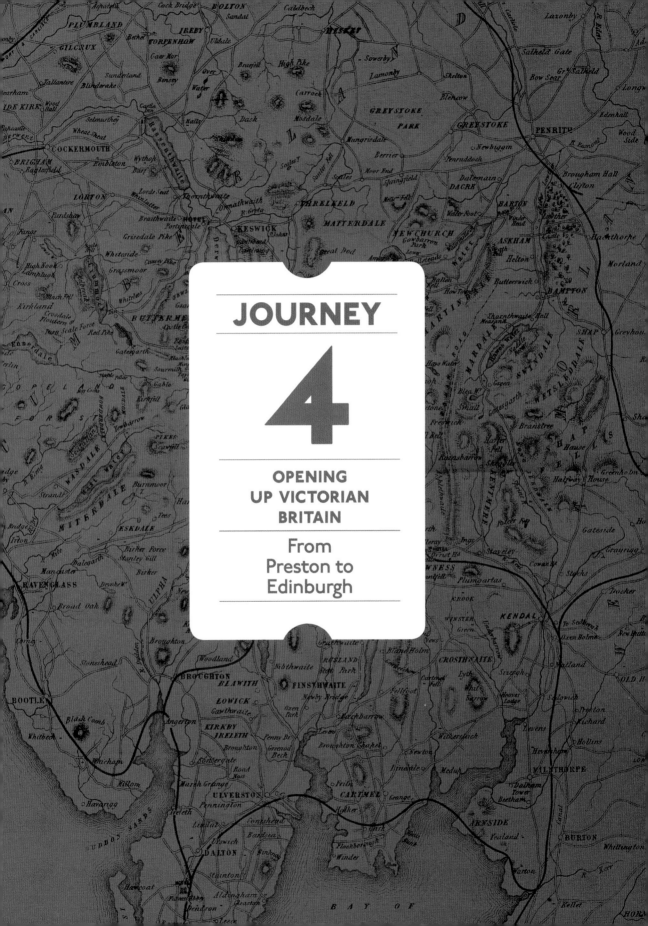

JOURNEY

4

OPENING
UP VICTORIAN
BRITAIN

From
Preston to
Edinburgh

Our next journey took us north on the first rail link between England and Scotland. Until the railways came, the communities of north-west England were almost impenetrable, as the hilly terrain kept road building to a minimum. For better or worse, this route helped open up remote areas of Britain, notably the Lake District and the Yorkshire Dales.

Our first stop was Preston, which is described by Bradshaw as 'One of the principal manufacturing towns of the country. There are upwards of 50 cotton mills in this town.' He goes on to say: 'The commercial annals of this town are memorable for two long continued disputes between the employers and employed.'

Presumably he is alluding to the 1842 riot by cotton workers protesting about the conditions in the mills that ended in four deaths after armed troops opened fire. Twelve years later there was a strike by cotton workers that lasted for more than 25 weeks. Clearly Preston was notorious for its poor industrial relations record.

In Bradshaw's day, Preston's residents also had a reputation for hard drinking, which may explain why it became the home of the British Temperance Movement in 1832, founded by former weaver and cheese entrepreneur Joseph Livesey (1794–1884). The Liverpool-born Livesey believed that alcohol was the root of all social ills, seeing it as a cause rather than a symptom of the abject poverty suffered throughout industrial heartlands.

Cheap travel helped the teetotal movement to mushroom, as trains transported hundreds and eventually tens of thousands of people to Temperance rallies to hear the charismatic Livesey speak. Although Britain stopped short of outright prohibition of alcohol, as was introduced throughout the United States in the early twentieth century, it was estimated that during Livesey's day one in 10 people chose to abstain from drink, a figure that peaked during the First World War when new licensing laws reduced pub opening times.

The next part of our journey took us 20 miles west from Temperance Preston to the coast, and we travelled on the *Blackpool Belle*, better known to countless young lovers as the passion wagon. Blackpool and its bright lights was such a popular destination with young people that the railways ran special services every weekend from other northern towns, operating late into the night.

RIGHT: **FAMILIES MADE THE MOST OF BLACKPOOL'S EXTENSIVE SANDS AFTER THE RAILWAY OPENED THERE AS EARLY AS 1846.**

OVERLEAF: **AFTER BLACKPOOL TOWER OPENED IN 1894, THE RESORT – UNRIVALLED FOR ATTRACTIONS – WAS A FIRM FAVOURITE WITH EVERYONE IN THE NORTH WEST.**

Norman and Norma Watkins began their romance on the *Blackpool Belle* in the 1950s. Norman remembers how, at the end of a night as the trains slipped out of Blackpool station, the light bulbs would be unscrewed to cast the carriages into a romantic blackout. There was darkness until the train approached their home town of Chorley, when all the light fitments would be returned to their rightful places.

The Blackpool of today is not so different from the one Norman and Norma remember. In Bradshaw's day, however, it was just starting life as a seaside resort and looked nothing like the Las Vegas of Lancashire that it is now. The guidebook describes it as a 'pretty bathing place on the Irish Sea … much frequented by visitors … in 1863 a new pier was opened which forms a most pleasant promenade'.

Bradshaw's Blackpool had a permanent population of about 3,500, but that was soon to change. With the railways that reached Blackpool in 1846 came thousands of holidaymakers, and within a matter of a few years, theatres, the winter gardens and three piers had been built. In 1879 almost 80,000 people came to see the first illuminations. They were marketed as 'artificial sunlight' and have been attracting visitors ever since.

In 1894 another great Blackpool attraction opened, at a cost of £42,000. Early visitors to Blackpool Tower, a half-sized replica of the Eiffel Tower in Paris, were charged sixpence to travel more than 500 feet to the top. Terrifyingly, the last stretches had to be done on ladders. Today the maintenance team, known as stick men, still use ladders daily. From the top it is possible on a clear day to see a panorama that encompasses swathes of Lancashire, the Isle of Man, North Wales and the lower ground of Cumbria. Even at today's peak summer prices it's still well worth the entry fee.

From Blackpool we headed north on another branch line towards Morecambe Bay and a station with the most splendid view out across the sands. In the nineteenth century Morecambe Bay was an isolated area comprising small shellfishing villages. As the trains made it more accessible, the fresh cockles, prawns, shrimps and lobsters were soon being whisked to Manchester fish market.

Bradshaw is very clear about the dangers of the bay: 'Morecambe is a fine sheet of water, eight or 10 miles wide, when the tide is up: but at low tide its quick sands are extremely treacherous and must on no account be crossed without the guide who is paid by Government and carries you over in a cart.'

Incredibly, 160 years on, there is still an official guide, paid by the state, who lives near the remote station of Kent's Bank watching over the enormous mudflats. Cedric Robinson is the current incumbent of a job that dates back to the sixteenth century and is held for life. It became a royal appointment after scores of lives were lost at a time when local people had no choice but to brave the ever-changing sands on foot or by cart. For the annual salary of £15 and the cottage he lives in, every fortnight or so Cedric conducts tours across the treacherous sands for walkers, sometimes taking more than 100 people, and marking the route with laurel branches.

Morecambe Bay hit the news in 2004 when at least 21 Chinese cockle pickers tragically drowned in a racing tide. Cedric knows well that the 200 square miles of sands are perpetually shifting and are licked by a tide that comes in so quickly that you can't outrun it. The tide never tires, Cedric warns. There's also the threat of quicksand, which he has seen swallow tractors and horses. The trick, he says, is not to stop moving and, if you get into trouble, to lie on the sands and roll rather than walk.

The next leg of our journey took us on a detour inland to Settle, starting point of the famous line to Carlisle via Ribblehead, Dent and Garsdale. This line hadn't even been built when our guidebook was written, but it was supposed to be one of the prettiest rail journeys in Britain, scything through northern Britain's limestone and black marble landscape. It was also a journey that we could only take because in 1989 Michael convinced Prime Minister Margaret Thatcher not to approve its closure. At the time Settle was at the centre of a campaign to save the threatened line. Now Michael was returning for the first time in 20 years.

This spectacular Midland Railway line was opened in 1876. Stretching 72 miles, and passing nine tiny stations and through some of the most rugged countryside in Britain, it is a magnificent piece of railway architecture with stunning viaducts and bridges.

It is a pleasure to travel this way through the Yorkshire Dales but, passing through its tunnels and over its viaducts, one wonders how the Victorians ever came to build it. The reason was that the Midland Railway Company was driven by the desire to have a high-speed line that would compete successfully with its rivals. The company's solution was to build straight across the Dales, with little thought for some of the details, such as the safety of construction workers. It took 6,000 men six years, working in miserable conditions, to complete the job.

RIGHT: **GUIDED TOURS FOR HUNDREDS OF WALKERS ARE CONDUCTED OVER THE HAZARDOUS SANDS OF MORECAMBE BAY.**

OVERLEAF: **THE BUILDING OF THE STRIKING RIBBLEHEAD VIADUCT CAUSED MISERY FOR HUNDREDS OF LABOURERS WHO RISKED DISEASE, STARVATION AND EXPOSURE TO COMPLETE THE JOB.**

A hundred years later, in the early 1980s, the Settle & Carlisle line was carrying just a few trains each day; passenger numbers were low; stations along the way had already closed and the route was losing money. What's more, the line was falling into disrepair and British Rail argued that it would now cost too much to maintain. Crucially, the magnificent Ribblehead Viaduct was in danger of crumbling, and British Rail estimated it would cost between £7 and £9 million to repair. It was a major plank in their argument for closing the line.

Tony Feschini, a former British Rail engineer, was employed to inspect the structure. After carrying out trial repairs, Tony was convinced that the viaduct could be saved for a fraction of the price, estimating it would only cost between £2,750,000 and £3,250,000.

Still British Rail mooted closure, but the idea was met with a storm of protest and a lively six-year campaign got underway to increase the numbers using the line, so making it more profitable.

As the crusade generated publicity, more people became rail travellers and the case for keeping it open strengthened. By the time a decision was needed some 300,000 people were buying tickets annually. As Transport Minister, Michael was able to show Margaret Thatcher that it was not only an important line in terms of history and heritage, but also a viable economic proposition. She agreed and, in April 1989, British Rail's request for closure was turned down. Since then, yet more people have started using the line and it now carries upwards of 750,000 passengers a year. For Michael, keeping the line open remains the achievement that he is most proud of from his time in Government.

Two thousand men, a third of the workforce for the whole line, took four years to complete the enormous structure at Ribblehead, with its 24 arches spanning 440 yards across the valley. The tops of the arches are 104 feet from the valley bottom and, despite some limestone cladding, the viaduct is vulnerable to some of England's worst weather.

For the repairing of the Ribblehead Viaduct modern machinery was used. Back in 1869, when work on the viaduct began, the technology available didn't extend much beyond pickaxes and dynamite. The navvies who built it travelled with their families, and ill-equipped shanty towns appeared along the route.

Many lost their lives to smallpox and starvation. At the tiny church of St Leonard's in the hamlet of Chapel-le-Dale, historian Gerald

FOR MICHAEL, KEEPING THE LINE OPEN REMAINS THE ACHIEVEMENT THAT HE IS MOST PROUD OF FROM HIS TIME IN GOVERNMENT

OVERLEAF: **STEAM BOAT WAS A POPULAR METHOD FOR NAVIGATING THE LAKES – THE 'LADY OF THE LAKE' CARRIED PASSENGERS ACROSS CONISTON WATER UNTIL 1939.**

Tyler revealed that 201 people were buried there within five years and, of those, 110 were aged below 13. So many people lost their lives that the railway company paid for the graveyard to be extended. Even that wasn't enough and, at the far end of the graveyard, dozens of bodies lie in unmarked graves.

Even when the railway was complete, there was the job of keeping it open in severe weather. At Dent, which has the highest station in England at 1,150 feet above sea level, maintaining the line proved almost as difficult as building it. Fifteen men lived beside Dent station in winter, with the job of trying to keep the line free from snow. Workers came for six weeks at a time, isolated and packed like sardines into the small snow huts built in 1885.

The huts are still there today, but have been converted into luxury accommodation for tourists, reflecting the evolving fortunes linked to the railway. Dent station – some distance from the village – was closed in 1970. However, the campaign to keep the line open re-ignited the

tourist trade. With more frequent trains, Dent and other stations re-opened in 1986 and are thriving today.

After the Settle to Carlisle detour, we rejoined the West Coast Main Line heading into the Lake District. Bradshaw was so enamoured of the area that he suggested a variety of different tours according to how much time one had.

In the early nineteenth century poets including William Wordsworth (1770–1850) and Samuel Coleridge (1772–1834) lived in the Lake District and made it popular amongst the educated elite through their writings. Wordsworth, however, didn't welcome tourists to his paradise, believing the poor and ill-educated would not benefit 'mentally or morally' from a visit. So the arrival of the railways in 1847 was hugely controversial among those like him who wanted to maintain the area's isolation. And there's no doubt the onslaught of visitors was in some ways costly.

For the traveller arriving by train Bradshaw promised an immediate delight: 'From Windermere station the lake appears in view, with its beautiful islands and grassy well wooded fells around its borders.' These days it has become so built up that you struggle to even get a glimpse of the lake. To attract more visitors the railway company had changed the name of the station from Birthwaite to Windermere, and the station is still there – only these days it houses a supermarket.

Bradshaw next suggests a trip out on to the lake, and that at least is one of the original delights still available to trippers. All but gone are the days when you could dip a kettle into crystal-clear lake waters to brew a cuppa. One of the major downsides of mass tourism has been the rising levels of pollution in the lake, caused by sewage overflow. Things are better at the north end, where the lake is fed by freshwater tributaries.

John Pinder, from the Environment Agency, monitors the water quality, particularly the level of phosphates found in sewage and fertilisers that stimulate massive growths of algae. As the algae blooms die, they take oxygen out of the water, reducing its quality. For the last two years John has been working with the whole community on trying to clean up the lakes.

Although it was the trains that brought the huge numbers of people to the lakes, all armed with their Bradshaw, he wasn't the first person to promote the area. Ironically, the reluctant Wordsworth – who was Poet Laureate from 1843 and a vigorous campaigner against the railways –

ALL BUT GONE ARE THE DAYS WHEN YOU COULD DIP A KETTLE INTO CRYSTAL CLEAR LAKE WATERS TO BREW A CUPPA

GRAZING IN THE SHADOW OF A LAKELAND FELL, HERDWICK SHEEP ARE NATIVE TO CUMBRIA WHERE THEY THRIVE ON RICH GRASSLANDS WATERED BY FREQUENT RAIN.

has inadvertently done more to attract visitors than anyone else. Now his grave, in St Oswald's Church at Grasmere, is a tourist attraction in its own right.

There was another, less obvious spin-off from the arrival of the railways. Farms that used to supply only their local markets suddenly became national enterprises as their produce was whisked away by rail. In the nineteenth century railway companies not only transported animals but owned the markets where the cattle and farm produce were sold.

Peter Gott's family has been farming Herdwick sheep, which are native to Cumbria, since the seventeenth century. As demand for fresh food grew, farms became bigger, and by the middle of the twentieth century the land was being farmed on an industrial scale. But farmers like Peter became conscious of having to compromise on quality. Now he is part of the slow food movement, which advocates small-scale, sustainable farming involving fewer food miles and resulting in more flavour on the plate.

THE BORDER BETWEEN ENGLAND AND SCOTLAND DID NOT HOLD FIRM UNTIL AFTER THE BATTLE OF CULLODEN WHEN THE LARGELY SCOTTISH FORCE LED BY BONNIE PRINCE CHARLIE WAS SLAIN.

Nowhere outside the Lake District will you find this type of sheep, with its own distinct flavour, raised on old-fashioned herbage in the fells. It is nonetheless very tough to run a small farm, so Peter has had to diversify to keep afloat, producing pies and 30 varieties of his own speciality sausages.

From the lakes, our journey took us further north via Penrith into the Border country and to Carlisle. When the railways arrived in 1847, passengers had to change trains there, making Carlisle one of the busiest stations in the country. Most, though, were simply passing through and never got to see the town itself. Those who did would have been struck by its degree of fortification.

Perhaps it's not surprising. The English and Scots battled for control of Carlisle and its castle for more than 700 years, until the last Scottish uprising led by Bonnie Prince Charlie came to an end at the Battle of Culloden in 1745. But that still left the marauding moss troopers, or Border reivers as they're known locally, for Carlisle to contend with.

Artist Gordon Young is a descendant of this forgotten people. He explained how, 400 years ago, the frontier between the English and Scots shifted constantly. Marching armies from north and south repeatedly laid waste to the area, making it difficult to govern. And the reivers operated within this no man's land, taking full advantage of its lawless state. They were skilled rustlers but often ended up taking anything they could carry. In 1525, in an attempt to bring the troublesome reivers to heel, the Archbishop of Glasgow laid a 1,069-word curse on them, which was read out by priests in every parish.

In those days men gave their allegiance not to their country but to their clan or family. And it wasn't just a case of the Scots raiding the English and vice versa. Feuding families brought bitter disputes to the same neighbourhood. Gordon explained that emerging from this tough, bloody place were dynasties whose names are now known the world over, including Irvine, Carmichael, Johnston, Dixon and Young. There have even been some famous reiver sons such as Richard Nixon and Neil Armstrong.

From Carlisle, the train crossed the River Eden and then the Esk on its way north-west to the Scottish border and, just beyond it, one of Scotland's most famous towns – Gretna Green. Even in Bradshaw's day Gretna was known for one thing. 'It has for more than 80 years been the place of celebration of marriages of fugitive lovers from England.'

'IT HAS FOR MORE THAN 80 YEARS BEEN THE PLACE OF CELEBRATION OF MARRIAGES OF FUGITIVE LOVERS FROM ENGLAND'

The marriage laws in Scotland have always been more liberal than those in England and, when the railways reached Gretna in 1848, the steady stream of runaway lovers turned into a flood. According to Bradshaw, more than 300 marriages took place annually here and in the neighbouring village of Springfield, and the fees varied from 1 to 40 guineas.

But Bradshaw was convinced the practice was coming to an end. 'An Act of Parliament has since come into operation which requires a residence in Scotland of too long a duration to suit the purpose of fugitive lovers and the blacksmith of Gretna Green, like Othello, will now find his "occupation gone".'

Of course, marriage is still big business for Gretna Green, with more than 5,000 couples a year tying the knot there. That's one in six of all weddings in Scotland, and a quick wander around the town makes it clear that it's something that keeps many people in work.

What's less well known about Gretna is that just a few miles down the track are the remains of a secret factory that played a crucial role in the First World War. No one had ever filmed before at what is still an MoD site. Inside we discovered a strange landscape of bunkers and hills built specifically to handle high explosives that were made and stored here.

Today David Watt manages the munitions factory, which came into existence after the Battle of Loos in 1915, when the army found itself critically low on shells. So low, David said, that Britain might have lost the war. As a result this huge facility covering hundreds of acres was built. Shells were made and packed round the clock by women mixing 'Devil's Porridge' – a paste of nitroglycerine and gun cotton that went inside armaments. At its peak the factory was producing 800 tons of it a week. Good wages were paid to the women workers, many drawn from domestic service, but there were multiple hazards from fire, explosions and the noxious chemicals being used. The women were uniformed and wore some protective clothing. The factory even had its own internal railway to carry the munitions around the vast site and the workers from their army-style barracks.

Our next train was substantially larger than the narrow-gauge MoD railway and whisked us swiftly past Lockerbie, Moffat and Lanark towards Glasgow. Even in Bradshaw's day Glasgow was famous for its rivalry with Edinburgh. 'The ancient city of Glasgow,' he asserts, 'is one of the most splendid in Europe and is not surpassed for beauty of

INSIDE WE DISCOVERED A STRANGE LANDSCAPE OF BUNKERS AND HILLS BUILT SPECIFICALLY TO HANDLE HIGH EXPLOSIVES

architecture in its public and private buildings, the length, breadth and elegance of its streets, squares and crescents, even by Edinburgh itself.'

Today the city centre still attracts the tourists, but Bradshaw used to encourage them to venture further afield. 'Glasgow itself is supposed to offer few attractions to the tourist but this is a mistake. Old Glasgow with all its dirt and discomfort ... is well worth a visit.' In a Victorian version of poverty tourism, he directed them to Calton, which was and is one of the city's most deprived areas.

In the nineteenth and early twentieth centuries, Calton – the weavers' quarter – was a wretched place. Cholera was a permanent threat, killing thousands every year. Several families were crammed into each small house. Today living conditions are better, but the area still has troubling social problems, including sectarianism rooted in Irish immigration during past centuries. Despite attempts to improve life here, such as the mass rebuilding of the 1980s, the life expectancy for an adult male is 55, decades below the national average.

DURING THE FIRST WORLD WAR WOMEN MUNITIONS WORKERS PRODUCED SHELLS AND OTHER ARMAMENTS AT GRETNA'S SECRET BASE.

Elsewhere the city is enjoying a renaissance. Sleek contemporary museums line the old dock. Grand Victorian buildings in the West End have been restored. Glasgow is a city that retains its civic pride, and that's reflected in how it has become a top tourist destination, welcoming 4 million people each year.

On the 45-mile journey towards Edinburgh through the Clyde Valley the scenery is less dramatic than that of Highland Scotland, but the farms are more abundant. Bradshaw was enthusiastic: 'A district of country rich in mineral wealth, beautiful scenery, celebrated far and near as the Orchard of Scotland and famous for its fine fruit.'

Scotland's cooler weather meant that fruit ripened there long after the season had finished further south. As the railways extended, there was wide demand for fruit from the lush orchards of the Clyde Valley. Picking was organised around the clock and the fruit would be sent on the early freight trains. Today, many of the orchards are neglected and overgrown, but there is a small group of people trying to revive the area's heritage varieties that might otherwise disappear.

It is difficult to see Clyde Valley orchards ever approaching their Victorian peak again, but they are beginning to rekindle their fortunes, offering fruit and juice which growers sell locally.

Soon we are at Scotland's grand capital, Edinburgh. The railway snakes through a ravine to Waverley station, with Edinburgh Castle looming above on an enormous rock that dominates the city.

Among its other claims to fame, Edinburgh boasts the biggest lost property office in Britain, receiving about 600 items a year. As well as the ordinary bags and umbrellas, people lose some bizarre items. Everything from a suitcase containing an octopus to a bag full of live eels has turned up on the shelves of lost property at Edinburgh station.

Edinburgh's first railway was not the line to Glasgow, surprisingly, but went instead to Dalkeith, about five miles to the south-east. On this line, which passed round the edge of Holyrood Park, the trains were horse-drawn, except for a steep incline inside a tunnel, where a stationary steam engine was used to haul the carriages.

In Bradshaw's description Edinburgh is labelled, not for the first time, a 'modern Athens'. But the book also mentions something altogether more mysterious. Bradshaw insists that, opposite the seventeenth-century Tron Kirk, lies a cellar where the momentous Treaty of the Union was signed. This key event, which in 1707 joined England and Scotland together

under one parliament, seemed to have taken place in what is now the ladies' loo in an Italian restaurant. The restaurant gets a steady flow of visitors asking the same question about the political history of the toilets, though probably not all thanks to a 170-year-old guidebook.

Dr John Young from Strathclyde University explained that Scottish politicians who wanted a union with England were jostled and attacked on a regular basis, so there was a possibility that Unionist politicians sought refuge in the cellars of what was then a house. Rumours soon circulated about the surreptitious signing of the treaty in this cellar, and these were repeated in various publications, including Bradshaw's, over the next 50 years. The truth, unfortunately, is far less compelling. The treaty was in fact ratified in the old Scottish parliament buildings on Parliament Square – and nowhere near the Bella Pasta ladies' loo.

The last part of the journey was a sentimental trip for Michael, following a route he had taken many times with his family that used to take him across the Firth of Forth. This was such an exciting journey for Michael and his brothers as children that they couldn't sleep as they waited in anticipation to cross the magnificent Forth Bridge.

As a boy in the 1880s, Michael's grandfather had rowed out to watch the building of this striking piece of engineering, Britain's first major structure in steel. The bridge took seven years to build and cost 75 lives. A mighty 55,000 tons of steel were used to build the bridge, and 8 million rivets bolted the sections together as it was assembled part by part before its completion in 1890.

It looks every bit as magnificent 120 years on. George Bradshaw didn't live long enough to see it built, but if he had he would have marvelled at the achievement.

Michael has seen the bridge from many angles, but one commanding view he had not enjoyed until now was from its very top. Ian Heigh, the man in charge of repairing and repainting the bridge, took Michael 367 feet above water level to look out from the top of one of the bridge's three great diamonds.

Ian is currently overseeing the massive job of blasting off all the old paint added to the bridge during its lifetime – the first time it's ever been done. The bridge will then be recoated using a modern paint with a much longer life. Afterwards it could be as long as 40 years before a team needs once again to perform the legendary, Herculean task of 'painting the Forth Bridge'.

MICHAEL PORTILLO ASCENDED
THE FORTH BRIDGE TO TAKE ON
A NEW PERSPECTIVE OF THE
FAMOUS STEEL STRUCTURE.

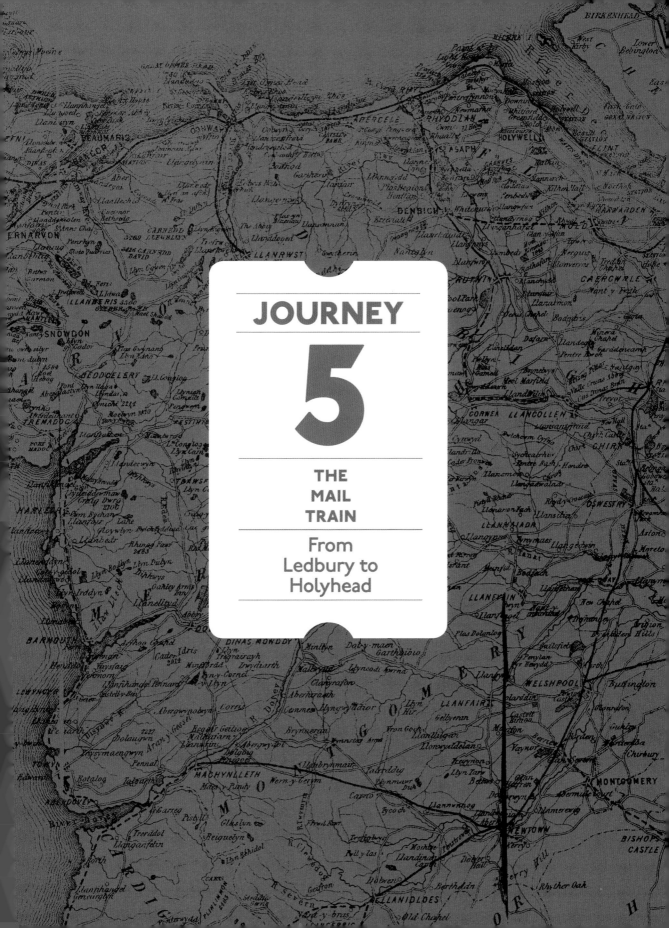

JOURNEY

5

THE MAIL TRAIN

From Ledbury to Holyhead

Many of the lines we travel on today were built to carry goods around the country, but the one heading out to Holyhead on the northern tip of Wales was created for a special kind of freight. It was to carry the Irish mail.

After the Acts of Union in 1800, which created the United Kingdom, it was incumbent on the British government to improve links with Ireland. The shortest sea crossing is between Holyhead, on the island of Anglesey, and Dublin. Clearly, Holyhead would be a pivotal part of any plans. Initially Thomas Telford (1757–1834) came to the rescue with the construction of the post road from London to the port there.

Despite the opening in 1826 of Telford's wrought-iron and stone suspension bridge linking Anglesey with mainland Britain, across the treacherous Menai Strait, the journey remained slow going. There was a golden opportunity here for the railway to prove its worth. The Chester to Holyhead line, built by Robert Stephenson to his father George's coast-hugging design, began construction on 1 March 1845. Chester station opened on 1 August 1848, the same day the first mail train reached Holyhead. The new and lofty Britannia Bridge took trains across the water to Anglesey. A journey that previously would have taken more than a day was cut to a matter of hours.

However, the outlook was not as rosy as the railway operators had hoped. The Chester to Holyhead Railway Company invested heavily in the route in anticipation of also winning the mail shipping contract to Dublin, but ultimately that went instead to the City of Dublin Steam Packet Company. Consequently the company struggled to get on a forward foot and was duly taken over by the London & North Western Railway Company in 1859.

Although the line was built to carry the mail, this historic railway brought change to all kinds of businesses along the route. We would be visiting some of them, but we decided to begin our journey further south, in the undulating countryside of Herefordshire, before joining the historic mail route in Cheshire.

Our starting point was Ledbury, a picturesque market town to the west of the Malvern Hills. Ledbury is best known today for its fine black and white timber-framed buildings, but Bradshaw describes it as a place 'remarkable for its manufacture of rope, twine and also cider and perry'. Perry is an alcoholic drink similar to cider but made from pears. One of the oldest commercial perry producers is still in operation just outside town.

PREVIOUS PAGE: **THE TUBULAR BRITANNIA BRIDGE WAS BUILT TO CARRY TRAINS HEADING FROM CHESTER TO HOLYHEAD ACROSS THE TREACHEROUS MENAI STRAITS.**

LEFT: **CIDER APPLES UNLOADED AT A BULMER'S FACTORY IN 1957. THE COMPANY HAS PROFITED FROM THE RESURGENCE IN POPULARITY OF PEAR CIDER IN RECENT YEARS.**

Helen Thomas's family have been making perry for 170 years and now sell a staggering 28 million pints per year. It was originally made for private consumption – like cider, it was traditionally part of labourers' wages in rural areas – though some was sold at the farm gate. Helen's great-grandfather, Henry Weston, began making it on a larger scale at his farm in Much Marcle, having noticed the growing popularity of drinks imported from across the British Empire.

When the railways came, Henry realised the potential for distributing his perry and started to produce it commercially. As the train network expanded through Herefordshire, Henry's business grew and he began processing and bottling other growers' pears. It wasn't long before Weston's perry was being sold all over the country.

Perry pears aren't the same as pears grown for eating. Furthermore each variety of perry pear has a different flavour. At Weston's they are using the same varieties – and often from the same trees – as Helen's great-grandfather in the late nineteenth century.

Another reason for the distinctive taste of Weston's perry is the way it is made. Helen still uses three enormous vats which Henry Weston bought years ago. The largest, known affectionately as Pip, holds around 40,000 gallons. Helen explained that, much like whisky, there are different grades of perry, along with single varieties and blends. The perry of Bradshaw's day was a flat drink, but later bubbles were added, giving it a similar quality to champagne.

Mention perry, and most people haven't heard of it until you mention its branded names like Babycham and Lambrini. But after being out of fashion for decades, it seems as though perry's fortunes are changing. Its beefier brother, pear cider, has become one of the trendiest drinks of the twenty-first century – while some maintain that perry and pear cider are in fact the same thing.

From Ledbury, our next train took us west towards Hereford along what Bradshaw described as one of the most picturesque lines in the country. It still is today, and as you speed through the rich green landscape it seems to encapsulate the very essence of the English countryside.

The reason for our next stop was to search out a local breed of cattle. Familiar for its white face and rich brown coat, and much admired by Bradshaw, Hereford cattle had become one of the country's most popular breeds by the nineteenth century. The Watkins family has been farming Hereford stock for five generations. Standing beside one of the many

MENTION PERRY, AND MOST PEOPLE HAVEN'T HEARD OF IT UNTIL YOU MENTION ITS BRANDED NAMES LIKE BABYCHAM AND LAMBRINI

branch lines closed in the 1960s, David Watkins and son George explained the enormous impact the railways had on farming in Herefordshire. Their arrival meant that George's ancestors' cattle could go straight from market to anywhere in the country in a matter of hours. It wasn't long before three trains a day were leaving Hereford station, all carrying cattle to London. They were also exported across the globe, and today the largest producers of Hereford beef are the United States and Uruguay.

The recent 'mad cow' and foot and mouth disasters decimated beef farming in the UK, but there has been a steady domestic resurgence, David said, during the last 10 years. Known for its succulent meat marbled with fat, the Hereford breed has become the product of choice for discerning customers. At the Watkins' Hereford hotel beef is hung for 25 days in fridges to tenderise the meat. As it gradually loses water, the taste is intensified.

One of the main reasons for the excellence of Hereford beef is the life these cattle lead, grazing in the fields. A diet of grass has now been proved to produce meat with a longer shelf life, a better colour and a delicious flavour, as well as containing an essential fatty acid. We also learnt that Herefords are probably descended from a Roman breed.

While we were in Hereford we wanted to find out more about something to which Bradshaw, in the entry for Hereford Cathedral, gave one short line: 'A curious Saxon map of the world is in the library.' The library is the biggest chained library in the world, and the map, of course, is one of Britain's most important medieval artefacts, the Mappa Mundi.

Drawn on one sheet of calf skin, probably by monks, this map reflects the thinking of the medieval church and thus places Jerusalem at the centre, with the rest of the world spreading out around it. Although it is geographically fanciful it remains an extraordinary work of art and scholarship, containing 500 drawings, including scenes from the Bible as well as classical mythology, and images of various peoples of the world.

Dominic Harbour, the Cathedral's commercial director, explains that the Mappa Mundi should be seen as a virtual map, conceptual rather than geographically accurate. Its purpose was to educate and underline the centrality of the church to everything, while today it has immense value as a thirteenth-century vision of the world.

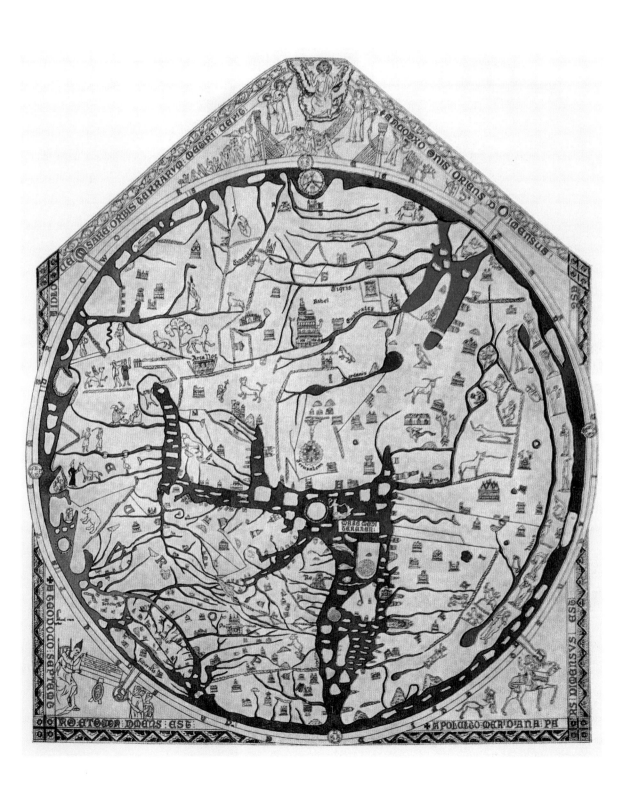

IN BRADSHAW'S
DAY THE RURAL
MARKET TOWN
WAS AT THE
CENTRE OF THE
INDUSTRIAL
REVOLUTION,
BUSY WITH MILLS
AND FOUNDRIES

Leaving the cathedral's great red sandstone tower behind us, we set off towards Shrewsbury, some 50 miles to the north. The line goes through the historic town of Ludlow, with its mighty castle, and threads its way between the hills of Wenlock Edge to the east and the Long Mynd to the west before descending into the Severn valley at Shrewsbury. Here it was industrial rather than medieval history that captivated us. In Bradshaw's day the rural market town was at the centre of the Industrial Revolution, busy with mills and foundries. Among the most important was Ditherington Flax Mill.

John Yates, Inspector of Historic Buildings for Shropshire, explained how this apparently ordinary building was at the very cutting edge of Victorian technology. It was the first iron-framed building, and its construction was, in John's words, 'an astonishing act of virtuosity, bravado and skill'.

All mills were mighty constructions, and Ditherington Flax Mill was no exception. It was 200 feet long, 40 feet wide and five storeys high. But, unlike its neighbours, it could withstand outbreaks of fire. Processing flax produced highly combustible dust, and fire was one of the great dangers for the industry. The cost of a blaze was in the order of £10,000, a small fortune in those days. So architect Charles Bage (1751–1822) was hired to design a mill that wouldn't burn down.

At the time the first cast-iron tracks were rolling off the production line in nearby Coalbrookdale, and Bage used the same technique to build cast-iron columns and beams. The clever design meant internal walls weren't necessary to give it strength. This subsequently allowed the factory owners to create large open-plan floors.

This system also enabled architects to create taller buildings – later using steel rather than cast-iron frames – in a design movement that eventually lead to today's skyscrapers. Without Ditherington Flax Mill the cities of the world would look startlingly different places.

One of the joys of reading Bradshaw's guide is the quirky information it contains. Take this extract from the entry for the Church of St Mary's in Shrewsbury. 'Many years ago a hair-brained fellow undertook to slide down a rope, laid from the top of this spire to the other side of the river. But he was killed in the attempt.'

Keen to discover more, we tracked down Robert Milton from St Mary's. At the top of the tower, looking out across the Severn, Robert told the story of Robert Cadman, a steeplejack who would supplement

DITHERINGTON FLAX MILL,
THE FIRST BUILT TO WITHSTAND
CATACLYSMIC BLAZES, IS
THE ANCESTOR OF TODAY'S
SKY SCRAPERS.

his income by performing high-wire tricks, cashing in on a craze for 'flying' that gripped the imagination of Britain in the 1730s.

Cadman was a master of the art, and it's said that he once slid down a rope from the cupola of St Paul's Cathedral in London blowing a trumpet. As his fame grew, hundreds of people would turn out to watch his performances, and his wife would collect money from awe-struck audiences. At St Mary's he walked up an 800-foot rope anchored in Gaye Meadow and ending at the top of the spire, performing stunts as he went. His finale was to slide down the rope from the spire to the ground, swinging by a wooden breastplate. But on 2 February 1739 the rope snapped where it was attached to the church and he fell to his death. At the church there's a plaque in his memory which reads:

Let this small Monument record the name Of Cadman, and to future time proclaim How by'n attempt to fly from this high spire Across the Sabrine he did acquire His fatal end. 'Twas not for want of skill Or courage to perform the task he fell, No, no, a faulty Cord being drawn too tight Harried his Soul on high to take her flight Which bid the Body here beneath good Night Feb.ry 2nd 1739 aged 28

After Shrewsbury we headed south-east to the village of Coalbrookdale, famous for its role in the development of the iron industry and now the site of a popular working museum of the Industrial Revolution. Bradshaw writes: 'Several important processes in the manufacture ... of iron have originated here ... in 1779 the first iron bridge was made. This still stands in substantial repair, at a point where it crosses the Severn with a single arch.'

Until the eighteenth century, charcoal was used to smelt iron, a process which required an enormous amount of wood to produce a tiny amount of iron. Then Abraham Darby I (1678–1717) developed a new technique, using coke hewn from the surrounding coalfields instead of charcoal. It meant that cast iron could now be made cheaply and in huge quantities. Iron manufacturing swiftly graduated from cooking pots to the first iron wheels and rails, the first iron cylinders for steam engines and, in 1802, the world's first steam locomotive, built by Richard Trevithick.

Eventually other products such as steel superseded this invention. Nonetheless cast iron has a striking monument to its success. Near

Coalbrookdale, where its component parts were made, the first iron bridge still stands proud today, in the village that grew up around it and to which it gave it's name. Built by Abraham Darby III (1750–91), grandson of the smelting genius, it is not only a masterpiece of engineering, but also an elegant addition to the natural landscape of the gorge it crosses. The bridge carried traffic until 1931, but is now reserved for pedestrians, who can gaze down at the historic stretch of river where the first iron boat was launched in 1787.

The technology of cast iron technology spread quickly. Among its early advocates was Telford, who was one of the most prolific civil engineers of the Industrial Revolution, building roads, canals and bridges all over the country. Thanks to Telford the aqueduct at Chirk, north-west

ABOVE: **SO INNOVATIVE WAS THE FIRST IRON BRIDGE, IT LENT ITS NAME TO THE TOWN IN SHROPSHIRE WHERE IT WAS BUILT AND BECAME A SYMBOL OF THE INDUSTRIAL REVOLUTION.**

OVERLEAF: **CHIRK AQUEDUCT, OPENED IN 1801, IS MIRRORED BY A VIADUCT BUILT SOME 50 YEARS LATER.**

of Shrewsbury, where the Ellesmere Canal crosses from Shropshire into Wales, became the first to be lined with cast iron.

For Chirk – already a stopping point on his mail road – Telford and his partner William Jessop designed 10 graceful arches that would carry the canal some 70 feet above the Ceiriog Valley, thus allaying concerns about industrial defacement of a delightful valley. He wavered about the use of cast iron and compromised by using it for the floor of the aqueduct. (Later a cast-iron trough was inserted to solve the problem of water leaks.)

Finished in 1801 at a cost of just over £20,000, it was a vital link between coalfields and granite quarries and the newly developing centres of manufacturing. In 1846 a viaduct was built next to it to accommodate the newly arrived railway. Together the constructions complement the majesty of the secluded valley, home of the kingfisher.

CHESHIRE PASTURES WERE ONCE ENRICHED BY BONE DUST TO PRODUCE VELVETY GRASSLANDS.

As the train continues through peaceful, rolling countryside it's easy to forget that this border was once a battleground between the English and Welsh. The castles along the way are the only reminders. Chirk Castle, just beyond the aqueduct, is described by Bradshaw as a 'noble looking edifice, which has been preserved from ruin and may be regarded as a perfect model of time-honoured castles of the ancient Lords of the soil'. He went on to call it a must for any visitor to the area, and in order to enable the Victorian traveller to make arrangements in advance for a visit he revealed it to be the seat of R. Middleton Biddolf Esq.

R. Middleton Biddolf Esq was no fan of the railways and did not relish the idea of the line coming across his land. But when he realised it was inevitable, he decided to make the best of it and negotiated for Chirk to have its own station.

Tourists flocked to visit the fourteenth-century castle with its tower and dungeon. Subject to numerous alterations since its inception, it remains the only castle built during the reign of Edward I that's been permanently occupied. Today it's the home of Guy Middleton and open for the public to enjoy most of the year.

Our next stop was Wrexham, nine miles to the north, and on our way there we travelled over more viaducts crossing the Welsh valleys. It's extraordinary to see how well they've survived the decades of pounding by the trains.

From Wrexham, we were heading towards the Cheshire pastures, another Victorian success story. According to Bradshaw, 'The famous Cheshire pastures were at one time almost worn out when they were renovated with bone dust and made five times as valuable as before.'

In the nineteenth century chemists began to identify the key ingredients of good fertiliser, and Cheshire became the centre of a huge experiment to use bone dust, or bone meal, to improve the grass. So successful was it that, over the next 100 years, the area became the centre of the dairy trade. Milk could be moved by train to nearby cities, along with associated products like cheese.

A rare farmer who still makes Cheshire cheese in the traditional way is John Bourne. John's family had been making cheese since the 1700s, but the arrival of the railways opened up new markets. By 1845 the farm was producing 12,000 tonnes of cheese every summer. At the end of the century it was making almost 30,000 tonnes. These days,

AS THE TRAIN CONTINUES THROUGH PEACEFUL, ROLLING COUNTRYSIDE IT'S EASY TO FORGET THAT THIS BORDER WAS ONCE A BATTLEGROUND BETWEEN THE ENGLISH AND WELSH

John produces cheese using hands-on rather than industrial methods, in much the same way his grandfather would have done. John's cheese spends up to six months stored in his cellar. As John says, the flavour is all in the maturing.

Now, to the west of Chester, as we join the original mail line to Holyhead, there's an excellent view of the Dee, the banks of which were once a hive of industry.

The railway bridge over the Dee was constructed by Robert Stephenson as part of the Chester to Holyhead railway and opened in September 1846. But a flaw in the design marred an otherwise glowing reputation. It was built using cast-iron girders strengthened by wrought-iron bars, and eight months after its opening it became the first railway bridge to collapse, killing five people as carriages from a local train fell into the river. As a result, bridge builders abandoned brittle cast iron in favour of more flexible wrought iron.

On its way towards the coast of North Wales the line hugs the south bank of the Dee estuary, which in Bradshaw's day was an area of heavy industry. The guide refers to 'extensive collieries, the coals from which are shipped to Liverpool, Ireland and various parts of Wales'. There's no sign of the collieries as you pass through today, but not far from the line there is another landmark mentioned by Bradshaw, Flint Castle, which he describes as 'but a mere shell, there being left only the grey ruined walls'. It's another in the chain built by Edward I to keep the marauding Welsh at bay.

For all its beauty, however, it was not the castle that drew us to Flint. Instead, we were heading to Rhydmwyn, to what was a top-secret chemical weapons factory in the 1940s. According to historian Colin Barber, Churchill had instructed the chemicals firm ICI to set up a factory in 1939, and Flint's remoteness, good rail links and proximity to ICI's chemical works at Runcorn made it the perfect location.

Colin explained that, although the use of chemical weapons such as mustard gas was officially banned by the Geneva Convention, they were made none the less, in case the Germans used them first and as a last-ditch line of defence should they invade our beaches. Tunnels, hundreds of metres long, were burrowed into the hillside to store thousands of tons of gas and chemical weapons.

Initially the work was done by men but, as the war progressed, more women worked on the deadly job of filling the shells. The most haz-

ardous part was adding the explosives and detonators to the shells, a job carried out in a section called the danger area.

Towards the end of the war, work started on an even more hush-hush project. It was here at Rhydmwyn that scientists first extracted Uranium 235, a key stage in the development of the atomic bomb.

A far cry from this dark history is the mood of our next destination, the Queen of the Welsh resorts – Llandudno. Since the arrival of the railways, this stretch of coast, which also includes Prestatyn, Rhyl and Colwyn Bay, has been a popular tourist destination. Llandudno's entry in Bradshaw's guide reads: 'This delightful place has become one of great import as a summer resort ... the air is particularly salubrious.'

Walking around Llandudno, you can't help but notice how well kept it remains. No faded paint and half-dead palms here. One reason could be that it has been controlled by one family for 500 years. Unlike

ABOVE: **FLINT CASTLE IS ONE OF A STRING BUILT BY EDWARD I TO KEEP THE WELSH OUT OF ENGLAND.**

OVERLEAF: **ATTRACTIONS INCLUDING ITS TRAMWAY MADE LLANDUDNO A CUT ABOVE RIVAL RESORTS.**

many landowners, when the railway came the Mostyn family saw the prospect of it running through their land not as a curse but as an opportunity. The Mostyns designed a purpose-built Victorian season resort laid out on a curved grid that matched the sweep of the bay. It has flourished ever since.

One of the most enjoyable things to do here is ride the Great Orme Tramway, one of only three cable-hauled street tramways in the world, whose cars take you high up on to the headland and offer some of the best views in town. It wasn't built until after his death, but Bradshaw would have loved it.

On leaving Llandudno for Conwy, just to the south, the Victorian traveller was advised by Bradshaw to prepare for another wonder of modern engineering skill, Robert Stephenson's tubular bridge, built to the specification of William Fairbairn (1789–1874).

This radical new design was constructed by welding together a series of wrought-iron boxes to make a tube. It was prefabricated on the shore and then hydraulically lifted into place in just nine days in 1848. The innovative system allowed them to create a 400-foot bridge without any extra supports, and at the Conwy end the railway disappears through the town's medieval walls.

It was the first time an engineer and architect had worked side by side on the design of the railway. The intention not to spoil the historic town was largely successful, except for the decision to add medieval-style ramparts at each end of the modern structure in an attempt to blend it in with the castle – and the existing bridge – and proved rather clunky. At Conwy, as elsewhere, Stephenson was following in the footsteps of Thomas Telford, who had completed his suspension bridge there in 1826. Today there's a third bridge, perhaps not as inspirational as its predecessors, to carry cars.

For Stephenson, as for Telford, the building of the bridge at Conwy was effectively a trial run for the greater challenge of crossing the Menai Strait, more of which later.

Opened in 1863, the Conwy Valley line to Blaenau Ffestiniog runs south through breathtaking scenery. Bradshaw describes it like this: 'The vale through which the River Conway flows is remarkable for its beauty and fertility. Its luxuriant pastures, corn fields and groves are finely contrasted with the bleak appearance of the Snowdon mountain, which towers in frowning majesty above it.'

There are 11 stations along the route, all adopted by local people. And it's volunteers from the local communities rather than railway staff who look after them, rewarded simply with free train tickets. To catch a train, you simply flag it down. It's a system that has seen the service flourish.

Just over half-way to Blaenau lies Betws-y-coed, which in the 19th century became the first artists' colony in Britain. It was started by the leading landscape painter David Cox (1783–1859), who came here to paint and encouraged his friends to join him. When the railways arrived, the artists themselves became a tourist attraction, with people coming to watch them at work and visit the scenes like Swallow Falls, made famous by Cox's paintings.

Betws-y-coed was not originally on the line but was linked up with an extension completed in 1868. As a result the population, already boosted by resident artists, was further increased by tourists. Today the visitors are still coming in their droves, but the resident population has nearly returned to where it was when the railway opened.

It is still a beautiful area, but for an abrupt interruption in the view. On the way towards Blaenau Ffestiniog the train passes through a tunnel built in 1879 and emerges among grey mountains of slag. This is because slate was mined rather than quarried. Bradshaw talks about 2,000 hands being employed in hacking and splitting. In its heyday there were six working slate mines in the vicinity, and the railways played a crucial part in their development, transporting slate to Portmadoc to be shipped around the world, particularly to Germany.

Underground it was hot and dangerous work, lit only by candles or sometimes lamps. Men wielding heavy tools worked six days a week from the age of 12. They weren't expected to live into their 60s.

The First World War saw the mines closed. Although there was some resurgence in the industry between the wars, the mines closed again at the outbreak of the Second World War, during which they were used to store treasures from London museums.

Today the industry is a pale shadow of its former self. It has been hit by a flood of cheap imported slate. The slate that is produced now is still prepared by hand and is mainly used in special restoration projects.

In Bradshaw's day the slate left there bound for the port on what is now the oldest serving independent railway in the world. The Ffestiniog Railway, founded in 1832, required a lot of innovation to cope with the loads the trains had to carry through such steep terrain. Finished in

WHEN THE RAILWAYS ARRIVED, THE ARTISTS THEMSELVES BECAME A TOURIST ATTRACTION, WITH PEOPLE COMING TO WATCH THEM AT WORK

1836, the narrow-gauge line was designed to deal with the sharp corners. In those days it was powered by gravity, with wagons coasting downhill to the sea at Portmadoc. Horses were then used to drag the empty wagons back up.

In 1863 steam locomotives finally replaced horses for the uphill leg of the operation. The railway company also pioneered a kind of double engine powerful enough to haul the heavy slate trains through the steep mountains.

The last slate train left in 1946 but, eight years later, the line reopened as a heritage route carrying tourists between Blaenau Ffestiniog and Portmadoc. It is a spectacular railway with stunning views as it takes you down to the sea.

Before heading back to the main line towards Holyhead, we followed Bradshaw's recommendation and made a minor detour to Mount Snowdon, the highest mountain in England and Wales at 3,560 feet. To visit the mountain he suggests that you should hire ponies and guides.

ABOVE: **AN INDUSTRIAL ROUTE HAS TURNED INTO A HERITAGE TRAIL THANKS TO THE FFESTINIOG RAILWAY, ONE OF THE OLDEST IN EXISTENCE.**

OVERLEAF: **A RACK AND PINION TRAIN COPES ADMIRABLY WITH THE SLOPES OF MOUNT SNOWDON, FERRYING LESS ABLE OUTDOOR TYPES UP AND DOWN.**

Today the best option to get you up there is a stout pair of legs. However, for the less sturdy, since 1894 there's been a railway running from Llanberis almost to the top.

The line is so steep that a normal friction railway would run back down the hill, so the trains use a Swiss system called rack and pinion. Between the tracks is a rack of teeth, with which a pinion or cog wheel on the train meshes, thus preventing the train from sliding down the track. It is the only such railway in Britain.

Travelling at a very sedate 6.5 miles per hour, the train gets to the summit in just 50 minutes. At the top you can see the remains of stables and two hotels, a reminder of what a very different experience the ascent would have been before the railways arrived.

The Victorians were great explorers, especially when it came to nature. To help them, Bradshaw's guide lists several types of rare flower to look out for on Snowdon. But as ecologist Dr Barbara Jones pointed out, they didn't just seek and find. They arrived in their droves to pluck and preserve. Some species, like the mountain lily, became even rarer as a result, but thankfully it and many others are now protected by law.

Back on the main line, we headed on towards Bangor and, beyond it, another of those incredible feats of Victorian engineering, Robert Stephenson's famous Britannia Bridge across the Menai Strait. Both the bridge and the station by it on the other side are memorable, although for different reasons.

The station is Llanfairpwllgwyngyllgogerychwyrndrobwllllantysiliogogogoch, which has a whopping 58 letters (51 if you're using the Welsh alphabet). The name only dates from the middle of the nineteenth century, and there's a theory that it was created by villagers in a bid to embarrass the trippers who already inundated the area. The longest place name in Europe, it has in fact turned the station, which had little else to offer, into one of the most popular tourist attractions in Wales. The translation is something like this: 'Saint Mary's Church in the hollow of the white hazel near a rapid whirlpool and the Church of St Tysilio of the red cave'. Busy people tend to use the alternative name of Llanfair PG.

The bridge had Bradshaw almost lost for words. 'This magnificent structure was made to carry the Chester and Holyhead Railway across the Menai Strait. Like the beautiful bridge at Conway, it is on the tubular

BOTH THE BRIDGE AND THE STATION BY IT ON THE OTHER SIDE ARE MEMORABLE, ALTHOUGH FOR DIFFERENT REASONS

principle, but on a much grander scale, and is one of the most ingenious, daring and stupendous monuments of engineering skill which modern times have seen attempted ... we may justly express our admiration of it by calling it Mr Stephenson's chef d'oeuvre, but this would scarcely do justice to the remarkable bridge or its great architect.'

Sadly, much of the original Britannia Bridge, including its train tube, was destroyed in a fire in 1970. The replacement has a road bridge above the rail link. The great limestone lions that used to stand either side of the entrances to Stephenson's old bridge are still on guard, but they have had to suffer the indignity of being set below the level of the road.

The final stop on this journey is at Holyhead. On the mail route from London to Dublin this was the point of departure across the Irish Sea. 'The once small town of Holyhead,' wrote Bradshaw, 'will speedily become an important place.'

It did. When the railways arrived here in 1848 bringing the mail, they brought people too. Irish immigrants, British soldiers and politicians from all sides took advantage of the quick and easy ride to Dublin. Almost 200 years later, Holyhead may have lost some of that importance, but its port is still used by more than two million passengers each year.

EUROPE'S LONGEST STATION NAME IS CARRIED SHOULDER HIGH TO ITS RESTING PLACE.

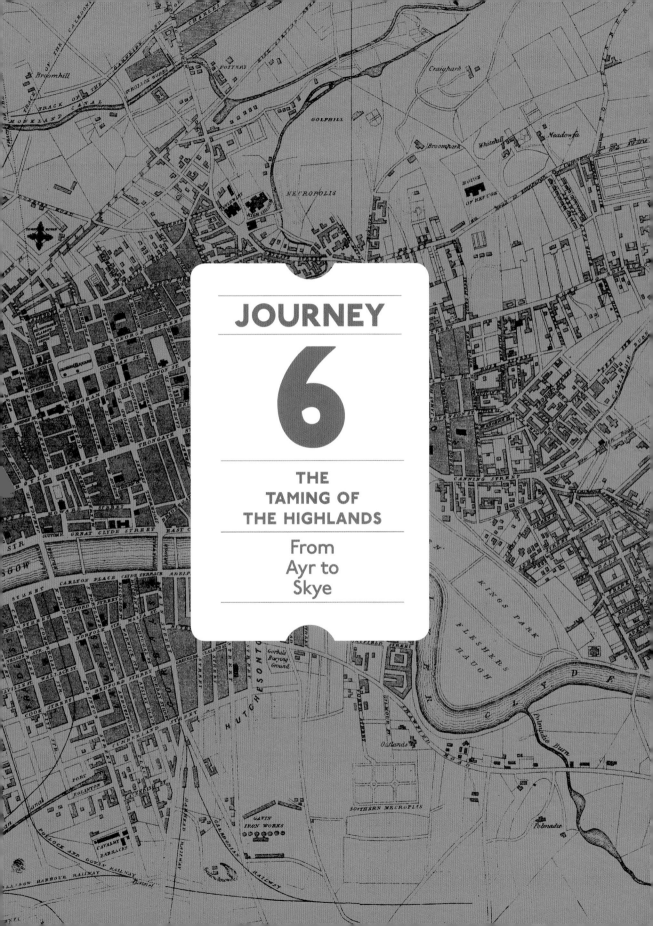

JOURNEY
6

THE
TAMING OF
THE HIGHLANDS

From
Ayr to
Skye

n the nineteenth century the Scottish west coast was a land of forestry and fishing, heather and haggis, wilderness and whisky. Life in what was frequently hostile terrain was continuing much as it had for centuries – until the arrival of the railway. The iron road was late in reaching its tentacles through the Highlands. Indeed, it was one of the most challenging stretches of line to confront railway builders of the age. Extreme gradients, curves, bogs and scree left engineers scrambling around for ideas. However, all the problems in the path of the ambitious project were finally resolved, and in October 1889 the first earth in the new 101-mile line was shifted with a silver spade. It took another five years and the labours of 5,000 men before the Glasgow to Fort William section of the line carried its first steam locomotive, pulling claret-coloured carriages. By April 1901 the leg to Mallaig – the first subsidised stretch in Britain – completed the route to the sea, and perhaps the most adverse environment in the UK had been tamed.

Was it worth the effort? Today's appreciative travellers seem to think so. In 2009 the West Highland line was voted the most scenic railway journey in the world by the *Wanderlust* travel magazine, above the Trans-Siberian Express and the Cuzco to Machu Picchu line in Peru.

Although the West Highland line starts at Glasgow, we began our journey further south in Ayrshire, to take in more of the joys that west Scotland holds.

The main function of the railways originally built here was to transport freight. As Bradshaw observed, it was a region rich in natural resources: 'It has abundant mines of coal, freestone, limestone, iron, lead and copper, and from the great abundance of sea-weed which is cast ashore, vast quantities of kelp is made.'

By 1840 passenger services were equally valued and there were already five trains each day, in both directions, between Glasgow and Ayr. At the time first-class passengers were paying 2d, while second- and third-class fares cost 1½d and 1d respectively. Initially third-class carriages had seats but, on 15 April 1840, the railway's governing board declared that these should be removed. Later the same year it was decreed that third-class carriages should be hitched directly behind the engine, so the travelling poor would not only be standing but receiving a face full of steam and soot too. At the time 18 passengers travelled in each first-class carriage, situated furthest from the engine, with 30 in second class.

WITH THE DAWN OF THE TWENTIETH CENTURY CAME THE FIRST RAIL LINK TO THE SCOTTISH HIGHLANDS, READY TO SHARE ITS GLORIES WITH TOURISTS FOR THE FIRST TIME.

MONESSIE GORGE, INVERNESS-SHIRE, SCOTLAND

BY RAIL TO
THE HIGHLANDS

BRITISH RAILWAYS

At least some of those travelling to Ayr were going to pay homage to Robert Burns (1759–96), whose verse had captivated the nation. For the Victorians, famous poems and novels were an immense lure and there was an established Burns 'trail' that involved sites made famous in his works.

Bradshaw was so bowled over by Burns that he devoted three columns of his guidebook to the great man. 'Ayrshire is called the "Land of Burns" who was born near the town of Ayr and every mile we come to is consecrated to that poet's memory. Innumerable pilgrims from all lands visit these scenes, and the place of the poet's residence, to gaze on what has been charmed and sanctified by his genius or merely to have the satisfaction of standing beneath the roof where Burns first saw the light.'

Although he died aged 37, Burns crammed more into his short life than most people manage in their three score years and ten. He was born into a poor family and worked on the family farm as a boy. Unusually, he was also tutored and discovered a love of, and a dexterity with, language.

His first collection of poetry, entitled *Poems, chiefly in the Scottish dialect*, was published in July 1786, with the aim of raising the cash for a passage to the West Indies where he was planning to emigrate. Its immediate success – with 612 copies selling within a month – persuaded him to stay in Scotland, and his body of poems and lyrics in both the Scottish and English tongues grew.

Burns is not only remembered for his verse. He was an incurable womaniser and heavy drinker, who also earned enemies as he poured scorn on national institutions including the Kirk. His politics were, for the era, radical.

His life is marked annually on Burns Night, commemorated on or near 25 January, the Scottish bard's birthday. The menu usually involves 'neeps and tatties' (turnips and potatoes) with haggis, traditionally served to the sound of Burns's poem 'Address to a Haggis', beginning with the lines: 'Fair Fa' your honest, sonsie face, Great chieftain o' the pudding-race!'

Haggis was something of an everyday dish until Burns propelled it to the forefront of the Scottish consciousness. Although it is inextricably linked to Scottish tradition it is likely that the original dish came from France via the Normans or Scandinavia. For any culture it was a way of disguising cheap meat and animal innards.

LEFT: THE LEGACY OF ROBERT BURNS IS A BODY OF VERSE THAT BRINGS THE ROMANCE AND RUGGED NATURE OF SCOTLAND ALIVE.

OVERLEAF: CROWDS AT PRESTWICK GOLF COURSE DURING THE OPEN CHAMPIONSHIP BECAME SO LARGE AND UNWIELDY THAT PLAYERS COULD NO LONGER SEE WHERE THEIR SHOT HAD LANDED.

The Taming of the Highlands 177

Butcher Stuart Duguid, who owns one of the oldest butcher's shops in Ayr, still makes hand-tied haggis to a recipe of sheep's heart, liver and lungs minced with onion, oatmeal, suet, spices and stock. It is boiled in the sheep's stomach for an hour before being served. It is perhaps an acquired taste, and Bradshaw was guarded in his response to it. 'Though a heavy mess, some think it by no means disagreeable.'

Like haggis, modern golf is widely accepted as a Scottish invention. Its rapid spread in popularity was undoubtedly helped by the arrival of the railway in this corner of Scotland.

The golf club at Prestwick, just north of Ayr, which opened with 57 founder members in 1851, came hot on the heels of the rail link with Glasgow. One of a limited number of clubs in the country at the time, it hosted the first Open Championship in 1860. Eight competitors played 12 holes in the hope of winning a red morocco belt with silver clasps, worth £25. The victor was the great Willie Park of Musselburgh, who would go on to win the Open three more times.

BELOW: **TOM MORRIS WAS INSTRUMENTAL IN LAYING OUT THE COURSE AT PRESTWICK AND STRUCK THE FIRST BALL OF THE FIRST OPEN IN 1860.**

OVERLEAF: **SHIP BUILDING ON THE CLYDE WAS A WAY OF LIFE FOR GENERATIONS IN GLASGOW.**

Players and spectators used the train for easy access to Ayrshire's golf courses. Indeed, by 1925 there were so many people watching the Open Championship at Prestwick that the players had difficulty seeing the fairway. It was never held there again, but by this time golf in general and Scottish courses in particular were firmly established.

The line follows the coast for a while before turning inland towards Glasgow. At Paisley we encountered another Scottish tradition – tartan. In Bradshaw's day Paisley was 'a thriving seat of the cotton trade', famous not only for its distinctive fabric design but also for producing thread. In its heyday there were 800 looms weaving tartan in nearby Kilbarchen. But at Paisley we learnt that, with tartan, not everything is as it seems.

After the Battle of Culloden in 1746, the wearing of tartan was outlawed. When the ban was finally lifted 36 years later, tartan gradually became the thing to wear. Its high point came in 1822 when King George IV visited Edinburgh wearing full tartan Highland dress. A Highland ball was held where Highland dress was compulsory.

Now everyone wanted their own tartan, and in 1842 two brothers claiming to be the grandsons of Bonnie Prince Charlie published a book called *Vestiarium Scoticum*, allegedly drawn from ancient manuscripts, listing lost tartans and their clans.

Thanks to the book, sold at 10 guineas, everyone could track down any relevant tartan. It even contained tartans linked to the lowlands, where none had previously been known. The weavers who benefited from this could not have been happier.

The authority of the book was barely questioned. The fact that tartans had traditionally been linked to clan districts rather than families seems to have been overlooked. And it wasn't until 140 years later that investigations proved the book was a fake.

Even if the fiction had been detected, the truth would probably not have stopped the public love affair with tartan, especially after Queen Victoria and Prince Albert had their new and favourite home, Balmoral, decked in it in 1855.

After arriving in Glasgow, finally it's time to join the West Highland line on one of the world's most beautiful train journeys. Early on the line runs alongside the River Clyde, which was once the home of a thriving ship-building industry. Among the ships forged in this stretch is *Cutty Sark*, now berthed in London and the only surviving example of a tea clipper.

Cutty Sark was launched at Dumbarton in 1869, one of a new type of sailing ship with its iron frame and timber hull and masts that stretched 150 feet into the sky. With this combination she could exceed the speed of rival steamships. She was named after the young witch in Robert Burns's poem 'Tam o'Shanter'.

Builders Scott and Linton were bankrupted by the construction of *Cutty Sark*. She was completed by Denny's of Dumbarton, who later went on to build the world's first passenger turbine steamer and first hovercraft.

Other notable ships – among thousands built on the Clyde – include the Royal Navy battlecruiser HMS *Hood*, sunk in 1941 with the loss of 1,415 lives, the liners *Queen Mary* and *Lusitania*, and the Royal Yacht *Britannia*. It's an area that was once known as Red Clydeside for the colour of the prevailing politics. In the General Election of 1922 several hardline socialists from Clydeside were elected to Parliament.

Leaving industrial Scotland behind, the line heads north-west along the Firth of Clyde and through Helensburgh. Bending to the north, it runs alongside Gare Loch and Loch Long before reaching Tarbet station, where the glorious Loch Lomond comes into view.

In 1263 Tarbet witnessed an extraordinary feat. When King Haakon of Norway sent his invasion fleet to attack Scotland, several ships came up Loch Long. At the end of the loch the Norse crews proceeded to drag them out of the water and across the neck of land between Arrochar and Tarbet, before launching them into Loch Lomond and sailing on into central Scotland. King Haakon was later defeated at Largs on the Ayrshire coast.

This part of Scotland has become a popular tourist destination and another example of Victorian tourism driven by popular poems and novels.

It was Walter Scott (1771–1832), author of the 'Waverley' novels and generally regarded as the father of the historical romance, who put this area on the visitor map. His poem 'Lady of the Lake', set in nearby Loch Katrine, was published in 1810 and sold 25,000 copies in eight months. The novel *Rob Roy*, about a folk hero who roamed the nearby Trossachs, appeared seven years later and sold 10,000 copies.

The first to visit had to do so by coach. But when the railway arrived it disgorged many more people hungry to find out about the backdrop of Scott's masterpieces. A steamer trip completed their exploration of the literary landscape. Although his ponderous

writing style later went out of fashion, Scott did much to bring the Highlands into vogue.

Like vast areas of Scotland, this area was once covered by the Caledonian forest. Only a tiny percentage of the native woodland is left now, and railways played a part in its demise. At the village of Crianlarich, for example, where Glen Falloch meets Strath Fillan and Glen Dochart, the forest was stripped to supply railway sleepers. It suffered again with the advent of the First World War when timber was urgently needed to shore up the trenches of the Western Front. Meanwhile, on top of these sudden needs, wood was in perpetual demand for building and fuel.

A PASSION FOR THE TROSSACHS WAS INSPIRED AMONG TRIPPERS BY THE WORKS OF SIR WALTER SCOTT.

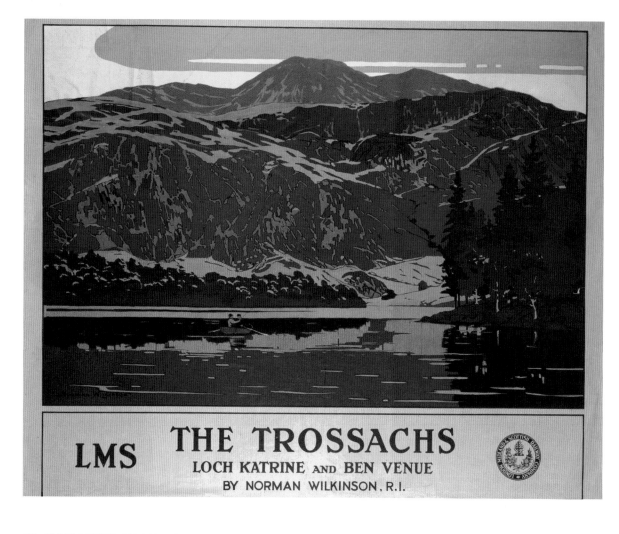

LMS THE TROSSACHS
LOCH KATRINE AND BEN VENUE
BY NORMAN WILKINSON, R.I.

In 1919 the Forestry Commission was set up and soon began replacing lost stocks of trees, using spruce seed from Canada. It's why there are numerous neat conifer plantations in evidence across the Highlands. Mature trees from plantations are used to supply timber merchants. For years it was transported to sawmills by train but, to save cash, the service was closed.

As the heavy loads of timber were subsequently transported by lorry, local roads began to suffer. Now there's a move – popular among local people – to reopen the rail service. A proposed terminal at Crianlarich would take 2,500 tonnes of timber off Scottish roads every week with just one train a day.

A more surprising industry is taking shape further up the line at Tyndrum, at the far end of Strath Fillan at the foot of the Grampians. A disused station building is the headquarters of a new company that's hoping to dig for gold. Chris Sangster, an Australian miner who set the company up, intends to bring 20,000 ounces of gold to the surface every year, representing profits of millions of pounds. He believes each tonne of rock mined there is likely to yield up to 10 grams of high-grade gold, worth about £200 and sufficient for a large wedding ring. It would mean jobs for a local economy that's in the doldrums.

Tyndrum owes its existence largely to mining. Lead was mined in the hill above nearby Clifton for 100 years or so from 1741. The nine-teenth century also saw a previous gold rush which brought an influx of people who duly built cottages for accommodation. But the price of gold fell and jobs were then in short supply. Optimists still pan for gold in the local rivers.

Tyndrum has two railway stations, which were built to serve dif-ferent lines. They are only a few hundred yards apart – but 10 miles apart by rail. Shortly before the village the West Highland line splits, with one branch going to Oban and the other to Fort William and on to Mallaig.

In fact it's not an original branch line to Oban but the remnant of a railway that preceded the West Highland line by almost a decade. The Callander and Oban Railway opened fully in 1880. It stopped carrying freight in 1965, the same year the portion of rail from Crianlarich east to Callander was closed.

Oban was still a busy commercial centre, as well as a holiday resort, home port for ships heading to Mull and many of the other Western

ONLY A TINY PERCENTAGE OF THE NATIVE WOODLAND IS LEFT NOW, AND RAILWAYS PLAYED A PART IN ITS DEMISE

Isles. It not only deserved a railway station, it needed one. So the line became a branch, to all intents and purposes, of the West Highland line.

Our battered old copy of Bradshaw was published long before the West Highland line was built, so for this section of our journey we needed to use a later edition. There it tells us that in the 1880s when the railway arrived Oban had a population of just 2,500. Today the number of residents still only numbers around 8,000, although that number triples in the summer with the arrival of tourists.

But it's not only the passenger ferries or indeed the merchant ships upon which the town is centred. It's the home of one of the oldest licensed distilleries in Scotland, and they have been making single malt whisky here for more than 200 years.

ABOVE: **THE SLATE QUARRIES ESTABLISHED BY JOHN AND HUGH STEVENSON IN OBAN HAVE NOT ENDURED IN THE SAME WAY AS THE DISTILLERY THEY STARTED, WHICH IS STILL PRODUCING SINGLE MALT WHISKY TODAY.**

OVERLEAF: **THE ISOLATION AND SOFT GROUND OF RANNOCH MOOR THREW UP NEW CHALLENGES FOR RAILWAY ENGINEERS, WHO ULTIMATELY BUILT THE LINE ON BRUSHWOOD.**

The distillery, dating from 1793, was established in an old brewery by brothers John and Hugh Stevenson, who also set up slate quarries, a tannery and a boat-building yard in Oban. It's changed hands several times since then but it's still a small operation, with two 670,000-litre stills used to produce only high-value single malts.

Back on the West Highland line proper it's time to cross Rannoch Moor, where the line is built on a floating causeway of brushwood. It was the only way engineers could cross the peaty plateau, which is both starkly desolate and stunningly beautiful.

The isolation of Rannoch Moor is difficult to comprehend. Certainly the team of railway surveyors who set off from here in January 1889 found it so. Seven men – among them engineers and a solicitor – set about their task with determination. However, they wore business clothes rather than rugged outdoor gear and carried umbrellas. Their pitiful kit was no match for the weather or the environment. Quickly disorientated, they were soon mired in peat bogs in freezing rain. One man fell and was knocked unconscious for four hours. He got to safety by following a fence which led to a cottage. The rest were saved by a rescue party made up of shepherds. A day later the moor was smothered in snow, and all would have died. Undaunted by their experiences, the party continued with the survey as soon as they were able. It wasn't long before accommodation was built for construction workers. Today it is a hotel and remains, bar the railway line, very secluded, being some 40 miles from the nearest garage and shop.

This section, like most of the line between Loch Lomond and Fort William, is single track. It means there must be special precautions to avoid head-on collisions. When the line was built a single token would be issued for the line section. The train driver in possession of the leather token knew he had right of way. Conversely, a train driver without the token knew something might be coming down the track.

Today it's an electronic token, transmitted by radio signal. It can only be 'released' by the train driver when his journey is completed. It means the line can be operated by few signallers with little infrastructure, so it is safe and cost effective. However, radio electronic token block, as it is properly called, is already obsolete and due to be replaced by European technology.

Corrour, which opened in 1894, is the highest main-line station in the UK. Its purpose was to serve the hunting lodge there. Owners of the estate had invested in the railway so that guests could make their

way towards this remote spot, before a carriage ride and a steamer trip brought them to their accommodation. For the rich it was ideal territory for hunting, shooting, fishing and stalking. While blood sports still play a part, estates like this are now usually more geared to conservation.

Bradshaw's guidebook offered the following description of what it called Inverness-shire but we know better as the Highlands: 'Its surface is in general extremely rugged and uneven, consisting of vast ranges of mountains, separated from each other by narrow and deep valleys. These mountains stretch across the whole country from one end of the island to another and lie parallel to every valley, rising like immense walls on both sides, while the intersected country sinks deep between them with a lake or rapid river or an arm of the sea.'

Among this impressive landscape lie the 'parallel roads', one of the great geological puzzles of the nineteenth century. Travelling through Glen Roy it's impossible to miss what appear to be three parallel roads that stretch as far as the eye can see. The roads form perfect contour lines, snaking in and out of the glen's irregular sides but – like tidemarks on a bath – maintaining precisely the same height throughout. Naturalist Charles Darwin (1809–82) felt sure the marks signified ancient marine shorelines. However, two years after he announced his theory, Swiss scientist Louis Agassiz (1807–73) countered it with another, claiming signs of a bygone ice age. Glaciers had formed plugs in the glen which had then filled with water. In 1861, after in-depth research of the roads was published, Darwin admitted he was wrong.

As Ben Nevis hoves into view it's impossible not to marvel at its dimensions. According to Bradshaw, 'Ben Nevis – the highest peak in Scotland or in the United Kingdom – is 4,406 ft above the sea and 20 miles around the base. The ascent takes three to four hours to the top, from which there is a grand prospect in clear weather.'

For Victorians it was a major draw. A pony track was opened to its top in 1883 and, after the railway reached Fort William in 1894, climbing the mountain became a popular pastime. Two women ran a Temperance hotel at the summit to cater for visitors. The following year a barber from Fort William ran up the mountain in the first timed ascent, giving rise to a series of hill running events. The Ben Nevis race is now a regular sporting fixture every September.

The pony track was created with a more serious venture in mind, however. On 17 October 1883 the Ben Nevis Observatory opened, funded

AMONG THIS IMPRESSIVE LANDSCAPE LIE THE 'PARALLEL ROADS', ONE OF THE GREAT GEOLOGICAL PUZZLES OF THE NINETEENTH CENTURY

by private donations, including one from Queen Victoria. It followed groundwork carried out by Clement Lindley Wragge (1852–1922), who climbed the mountain daily for sustained periods to make observations about the weather. The permanent observatory was a response to this endeavour by the Scottish Meteorological Society, which funded three staff there. Bravely they went out in terrible weather to take readings. Although the building closed in 1904 for lack of cash, the readings taken in the two decades it was open provided fundamental and comprehensive data on mountain weather.

Fort William, the next town on the route, sits on the eastern shore of Loch Linnhe beneath Ben Nevis and was once of major strategic importance. The stone fort held out against attack in both Jacobite rebellions in

BELOW: **BEN NEVIS IS A SIGHT OF UNPARALLELED GRANDEUR IN BRITAIN, ATTRACTING WALKERS – AND SOMETIMES RUNNERS – FROM ACROSS THE NATION.**

OVERLEAF: **GLENFINNAN VIADUCT POSSESSES UNEXPECTEDLY GRACEFUL LINES FOR A STRUCTURE MADE OF CONCRETE.**

BEN NEVIS

Britain's highest mountain · 4406 ft.

SEE SCOTLAND BY RAIL

BRITISH RAILWAYS

BRITISH RAILWAYS

the eighteenth century, but when the railway came in 1864 it was in the way and was demolished.

Beyond Fort William is the magnificent Glenfinnan Viaduct, across the River Finnan near the head of Loch Shiel, one of a number of bridges and viaducts that would carry trains onward to Mallaig – and the ferry to Skye.

Sir Robert McAlpine (1847–1934), known as 'Concrete Bob', took charge of the Glenfinnan project. McAlpine was a former coal miner who began his construction company in 1869. When it was announced that he was going to build the viaduct entirely of concrete, there were fears that the end result would be a monstrosity. However, the finished viaduct with its 21 arches, each spanning 15 metres, bearing a track some 30 metres above the valley floor, put paid to these anxieties. Not only magnificent but durable, the concrete construction has withstood atrocious weather for well over a century with few signs of wear. The viaduct is familiar to many as the one featured in Harry Potter films, used by the Hogwarts Express.

It was at Glen Finnan that Bonnie Prince Charlie (1720–88) raised his standard in 1745. He was the grandson of King James II, exiled after the Battle of the Boyne in 1690. James had been unpopular for being Catholic and pro-French and because he fervently supported the notion that he had a God-given right to rule. Thus his grandson expected at least Catholic and French support, if not divine intervention. Initially, when his standard was raised, it was only a few Highlanders that turned up. Just as hope was fading, some of the clans came to join him en masse, sufficient for an army that would take Edinburgh and embarrass the red-coated Hanoverian forces.

With Scotland conquered, many of his supporters were keen to draw a line under the lightning campaign, but Bonnie Prince Charlie wanted to take England too. With false promises of French support, he persuaded his men to go on. They got as far as Derby before a weary lack of purpose forced a retreat. The episode ended in the Battle of Culloden in 1746, the last to be fought on British soil. Although the Prince escaped, more than 1,200 of his men died in less than an hour at the hands of a vengeful English force.

Almost 200 years later, during the Second World War, the Highlands again became a place for fighting men to show unquestioning bravery. When ordinary armed forces were faring badly, Winston Churchill ordered the formation of an elite corps who would undergo rigorous training before being unleashed as a guerrilla force. Between Glenfinnan and the sea was one of the centres for this, Inverailort House. Here Simon Fraser, 17th Lord Lovat (1911–95), a celebrated commando officer, helped set up the first Highland special training centre. (One of his ancestors, the 11th Lord Lovat, fought for the Jacobites at Culloden, having changed sides, and was afterwards executed for treason.)

Inverailort was ideally placed as it was remote and yet enjoyed rail access to bring in men, equipment and ammunition. And the surrounding landscape, prohibited to the public during the conflict, was an ideal setting for war games – many of which involved live ammunition. Men were brought here from all over the country to master the black arts of hand-to-hand combat, knife fighting, sabotage, demolition, field work and survival skills.

Finally our rail journey finished at Mallaig, where the 'Road to the Isles' and the West Highland Railway both come to an end. But before heading home we boarded a ferry to Skye to pick up on an odd reference in Bradshaw. 'At Kilmuir … Florence MacDonald, the Prince Charles heroine is buried.'

After Culloden Bonnie Prince Charlie took refuge in the Outer Hebrides, hoping for a passage to France. Eventually he happened upon Flora MacDonald (1722–90), aged 24. Despite some misgivings Flora pledged her help and asked her stepfather, the local commander, for a pass to the mainland for herself, a boat's crew, a manservant and a maid named as Betty Burke. 'Betty' was in fact the prince in disguise. The boat sailed to Skye, after which the prince crossed to Raasay and boarded a ship for France.

Flora MacDonald was soon arrested, not least because local people had noticed that the gait of Betty Burke did not appear to be that of an Irish spinning maid. Flora was imprisoned in the Tower of London but was soon permitted to live outside its grim walls until in 1747, after a general amnesty, she was released.

Her act was one of charity, she insisted, rather than conviction. She later married and emigrated to America shortly before the War of Independence. After five years she returned to Skye, and on the voyage revealed her characteristic mettle by refusing to leave the deck when privateers attacked her ship. Her name resonates with the virtues of honour and courage that run like a thread through Highland history.

MALLAIG IS THE END OF THE LINE IN THE WESTERN HIGHLANDS AND THE GATEWAY TO THE ISLE OF SKYE, WHICH IS RICH IN ROMANCE AND FOLKLORE.

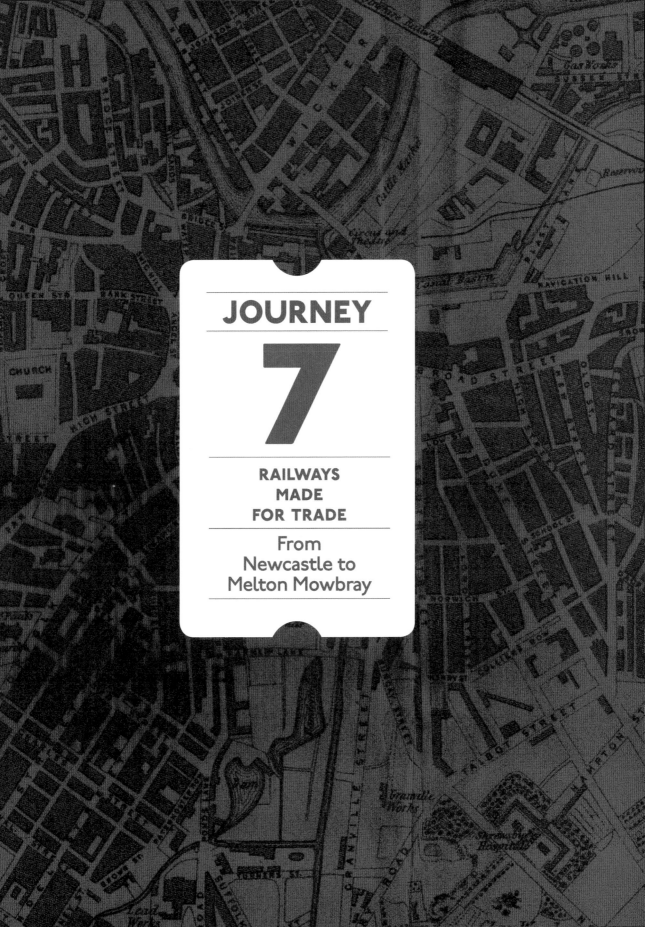

JOURNEY

7

RAILWAYS MADE FOR TRADE

From Newcastle to Melton Mowbray

For railway enthusiasts the journey to the north-east is something of a pilgrimage. It was here that George Stephenson (1781–1848), father of the railways, was born and brought up. And it's in this area that much of his pioneering work was done. Newcastle was already an important coal-mining area before the age of the train. Other early endeavours in the Industrial Revolution were also clustered in this northern corner of England. Although these enterprises preceded the railways, all benefited from improved transport links when they arrived.

Travelling between Newcastle and Melton Mowbray you're taken from industrial urban to distinctly rural, a stark contrast visible from a train carriage window. The railways transformed not only the cities, but the countryside as well.

George Stephenson was the son of a miner and before he became an engine man he worked in the colliery himself. His only son Robert was born into these humble circumstances too. One of George's earliest inventions was a safety lamp for miners, ultimately overshadowed by one unveiled by Sir Humphrey Davy at about the same time.

On discovering he had a talent for engineering he soon got into the business of building tracks and, later, steam locomotives. Until the coal industry was revolutionised by his inventions, coal from Newcastle was shovelled on to ships docked in the Tyne to be transported to London. Ultimately the train would do the job quicker and more cheaply, while rail also criss-crossed the complex of collieries, taking on some of the more back-breaking tasks. Nowhere was the invention of railway steam locomotives more welcome than among working men of the north-east.

Robert Stephenson who, unlike his father, enjoyed a formal education, joined with others to set up a family locomotive works near the station in Newcastle as early as 1823. It was here that Locomotion No 1, the first locomotive to operate on a public railway, was built. The Forth Street Works, as they were known locally, went on to export locomotives to developing railways all over the world. When he died in 1859 Robert Stephenson's company was the biggest employer on Tyneside.

For Bradshaw the might of the coal industry was something to shout about. 'Coal, the true riches of Newcastle, was first worked here in 1260 but the produce was scanty till steam power was used in 1714. Within a circle of eight to ten miles more than 50 important collieries are open among which are the Hetton, Hartley, Wallsend and other familiar

ROBERT STEPHENSON SHARED HIS FATHER'S FLAIR FOR ENGINEERING AND DESIGN, AND HIS COMPANY EXPORTED LOCOMOTIVES FROM NEWCASTLE TO ALL OVER THE GLOBE.

names employing 10,000 to 15,000 hands. High-main coal is got from a rich bed six ft thick, nearly 200 fathoms beneath the surface. The great northern field of which this is the centre, covers about 500 square miles in Northumberland and Durham and may be 1,800 ft deep. Many and various calculations have been made by practical men and geologists as to the extent of supply but all agree that it will take some hundreds if not thousands of years to exhaust it.'

The promise of job security proved false for mining communities. For one village in particular, perched on the sea cliffs near the mouth of the Tyne, the coal mining industry and the cliffs gave out long before the coal seams. Until 40 years ago Marsden was home to 700 people with homes, a school, a miners' institute, a Methodist chapel and a railway line with a station. The post office doubled as a general store and its

ST HILDA'S COLLIERY IN SOUTH SHIELDS WAS ONE OF NUMEROUS MINES IN THE NORTH EAST THAT OPERATED MORE EFFICIENTLY WITH THE BENEFITS OF NEW TECHNOLOGY AFTER THE INDUSTRIAL REVOLUTION.

front room was sometimes a doctor's and a dentist's surgery. Men from the village worked in the nearby colliery from its opening in 1878 until its closure 90 years later, after the surface coal was exhausted.

Amenities were basic. Returning black with dirt from a day's labour, the most a man could hope for was a bath in a tub in front of the fire. Once a week a horse and cart came to the village to collect the contents of the earth closets, while rubbish – at the time almost entirely bio-degradable – was tossed over the cliffs into the sea.

Food was grown on allotments or pulled from the waves. And it was the sea that once nourished the people here that finally proved to be their nemesis. Constant rock falls brought the cliff edge ever closer to the vil-lage. Anxious residents were soon complaining that they could fish from their back gardens because the sea was so close. Hopes that the small

DESPITE THE ADVENT OF THE MECHANICAL AGE, BOYS LIKE THESE WERE STILL EXPECTED TO GO DOWN THE PITS FROM AN EARLY AGE, SACRIFICING THEIR CHILDHOOD FOR THE SAKE OF THE INDUSTRY.

community would survive the closure of the colliery in 1968 were soon dashed when it became obvious the sea wasn't about to halt its forward march. First it became a ghost village. Now most of it has vanished.

Village and pit were built in the lee of Souter lighthouse. Opened in 1871 to protect ships from a notorious stretch of rocks, it was the first lighthouse to use a form of electricity. Its mechanics were designed by Sunderland-born Joseph Swann (1828–1914), who continued honing the uses of electricity until in 1879 he produced the first incandescent light bulb. Although it was decommissioned in 1988, the building with its distinctive red hoops still stands intact, fortunate to have been sited on the structurally sound Lizard Point rather than the adjoining cliff top. Today it's a tourist attraction owned by the National Trust.

Old Marsden was doomed, but it seems that in the future there may be hope for the coal industry at nearby Whitburn. Professor Paul Younger, an expert in the study of water pollution levels in former mines, believes the days of sending men down into the pits are long gone. Instead he is investigating ways of extracting coal cleanly, economically and safely with new technology. In layman's terms he suggests boring into the mineral seam, igniting the coal within it and using the heat that comes out to generate steam and electricity. Further, he envisages the carbon emitted in the process being captured and returned to the same borehole to be sealed up for ever. If these ideas become a reality they certainly could provide a stepping stone as the country seeks a carbon-free economy.

Given the dire consequences a mighty swell can have off this coast, it is perhaps not surprising to discover that the first lifeboat was pioneered at our next stop in South Shields. Bradshaw first alerted us to this fact. 'At South Shields may be seen, in the church, a model of Greathead's first life boat, invented and used in 1790.' Bradshaw is referring to St Hilda's Church and to boat-builder Henry Greathead (1757–1818), the man credited with the creation of a boat capable of rescuing stranded crews in high seas.

The quest for a lifeboat design began in earnest in 1789 after the loss of the *Adventure*, a Newcastle ship wrecked at the mouth of the Tyne. Thousands of spectators gathered to watch the demise of ship and crew, who fell from the rigging one by one just 300 yards from the shore. None of the horrified onlookers would take to a boat and attempt a rescue, as they were certain they too would be lost. Subsequently a

IF THESE IDEAS BECOME A REALITY THEY CERTAINLY COULD PROVIDE A STEPPING STONE AS THE COUNTRY SEEKS A CARBON-FREE ECONOMY

committee was formed which offered a prize for a boat design 'calculated to brave the dangers of the sea, particularly of broken water'.

A design by William Wouldhave, the parish clerk, was forged in copper, made buoyant with the use of cork. Its chief advantage was that it could not be capsized, but the competition organisers disliked the copper aspect of the model. Greathead's boat was made of wood but floated bottom up if it was capsized.

Wouldhave was granted one guinea for his idea, while Greathead was given the contract for making the boat. In the end he incorporated cork cladding from Wouldhave's model and further added a curved keel. It was rowed with 10 short oars and could carry 20 people. The 'Original' served for 40 years before being wrecked on rocks. Greathead went on to build more than 30 lifeboats, but his claim to have invented them was

PREVIOUS PAGE: **WAGONS ROLLED AT ST HILDA'S COLLIERY UNTIL ITS CLOSURE IN 1940 AFTER A 130-YEAR HISTORY, WITH 2,000 MEN EMPLOYED THERE DURING ITS HEYDAY.**

BELOW: **THE 'ORIGINAL' SERVED AS THE RESCUE CRAFT OF THE TYNE LIFEBOAT SOCIETY FOR 40 YEARS.**

challenged both by Wouldhave and by Essex man Lionel Lukin, who believed his drawings of an 'unimmergible boat' predated Greathead's by at least five years.

Lifeboats certainly played their part in the story of South Shields, because of its position. The unstable sandbars near the mouth of the Tyne proved a perpetual hazard to shipping. And it was shipping, along with coal, that made it a boom town. Its population increased from 12,000 in 1801 to 75,000 by the 1860s.

Its history goes back much earlier than that, though, and the banks of the Tyne are littered with Roman remains, including two very well preserved Roman forts, Arbeia at South Shields and Segedunum at nearby Wallsend. Moreover, Hadrian's Wall, built by the Romans to keep out the Picts of Scotland, is still evident here, although much of its stonework has been recycled in other projects including the thirteenth-century Tynemouth Priory. It wasn't until the middle of the nineteenth century that the first steps to preserve the Roman wall were taken. It is now recognised as a world heritage site, which means its stones can no longer be used for local road-building projects as they were throughout the eighteenth century.

Hadrian's Wall was not the only piece of heritage that was almost lost in the region. The tradition of rapper sword dancing is still alive and well in the north-east despite decades of negligible interest in it. It sounds like something modern, but in fact rapper sword dancing is so old its origins are unknown. It is surely related to other sword dances that are known to have existed in Yorkshire and across Europe.

It is widely thought to have had two 'revivals', the first when conditions for miners both above and below ground were grim. In the colliery village of South Hetton, for example, there were five water taps to serve 190 houses in 1842. Fifty years on and there was but one toilet for 154 houses. Living was hard, but the result was a close-knit community that sought to make the most of its limited leisure time. Rapper sword dancing, with its camaraderie and its competition, became an antidote to the misery of working life. The next revival came after the Second World War when a group of university students recalled the dances for public consumption.

The rappers are flexible lengths of steel – although in olden days greensticks would have sufficed. Moving to a fast beat, the performers dance acrobatically and wield the rappers with alarming speed, bringing

ALL THOUGHTS OF MINING MISERY ARE BANISHED BY THE SPECTACULAR SIGHT OF THE NORMAN CASTLE AND 900-YEAR-OLD CATHEDRAL

them together with loud clashes to form different patterns. The Forster family from the village of High Spen, just across the border in County Durham, are continuing a tradition begun in 1926 by ancestor Fred Forster, who taught a group of local children how to dance. A year later, calling themselves the Blue Diamonds, the group won the junior sword section of the North of England Musical Tournament. His grandson and other members of the family happily don costumes of nineteenth-century miners to perform the dances today.

With the onward journey to Durham, however, all thoughts of mining misery are banished by the spectacular sight of the Norman castle and 900-year-old cathedral, towering over a wooded horseshoe bend in the River Wear. Bradshaw says of Durham: 'From all the neighbouring points of view, its appearance is unique and striking and the public edifices exhibit a great degree of magnificence. The centre of eminence is occupied by the cathedral and the castle.'

Although the surrounding area had numerous collieries, Durham itself played little part in the Industrial Revolution. However, it had already

ABOVE: **THE BLUE DIAMONDS OF HIGH SPEN, JUNIOR CHAMPION RAPPER SWORD DANCERS IN 1927 AND AN INSPIRATION TO THOSE CONTINUING THE TRADITION TODAY.**

OVERLEAF: **DURHAM CATHEDRAL WAS COMPLETED BY THE MIDDLE OF THE TWELFTH CENTURY AND IS A PRISTINE AND MONUMENTAL EXAMPLE OF NORMAN ARCHITECTURE THAT HAS BECOME AN ICON OF THE NORTH EAST.**

been an important military and ecclesiastical centre for many centuries, as its fine medieval buildings testify. Its religious significance goes back to 995, when the body of St Cuthbert, 300 years after his death, finally found a permanent resting place. Durham became a place of pilgrimage, and after the Conquest the Normans built the huge castle and cathedral, from where the bishops of Durham wielded great power.

One episode of ecclesiastical history that is barely remembered now, but which may ring a few bells, concerned one of Durham's bishops in the middle of the nineteenth century, who was at the centre of an expenses scandal. Bradshaw identified the nub of it when he said: 'In 1856 an Act of Parliament was obtained to enable to Bishops of London and Durham to retire from their sees with handsome pensions.'

Already handsomely paid, the Bishop of Durham, Edward Maltby (1770–1859), asked for such a large sum that Liberal politician William Gladstone (1809–98) accused him of simony, or profiteering from spiritual things. Although the pensions were grudgingly agreed in

INSIDE DURHAM CATHEDRAL
THE DECOR REMAINS A TRIBUTE
TO THE ARMY OF ARTISANS
WHO WORKED THERE DURING
ITS CREATION, WITH ONLY BASIC
TOOLS TO HAND.

Parliament, the money Maltby received with his fellow bishop and his prospective role as statesman remained a matter for concern.

Hansard, the Parliamentary handbook, records a vitriolic attack by George Hadfield, MP for Sheffield between 1852 and 1874, on the subject, in which he refers to the two bishops receiving 'nearly £1,000,000 of the revenue of the church while there were 10,000 clergymen of that very church each receiving a sum not exceeding £100 per annum'. The injustice was not to be endured, he said, in a speech which came to this contemptuous climax: 'Would not the fact of these two right reverend Prelates, after having received nearly £1,000,000 from the state, and coming to the house and asking for retiring pensions to the amount of £10,500 a year, be canvassed in every pothouse in the country, and be made the subject of the song of the scoffer and the mockery of the drunkard?'

Today the amounts translate to an income of more than £67,000,000 paid while the Bishop was in post and £700,000 a year in the form of a pension. The MP's rage mirrors that of many over more recent stories of money-grubbing by elected and unelected Parliamentarians. In fairness, Maltby was the first regular bishop after a long line of 'prince-bishops' who wielded extraordinary power. Perhaps he expected financial recompense for waiving the right to raise an army, hold his own parliament and mint his own coins.

As the train head south, next on the line came Darlington, in North Yorkshire, a place of pilgrimage for railway historians. It was here in the 1820s that George Stephenson began laying rails to link the Darlington collieries with the river at Stockton-on-Tees. Opened in 1825, it is given the accolade of being the first purpose-built, locomotive-driven freight railway.

The Stockton & Darlington Railway began its life in 1821 the same way as any other, with an Act of Parliament. Its owner Edward Pease (1757–1868) initially conceived it as track with wagons drawn by horses like many others. But George Stephenson persuaded him that 'one loco-motive was worth 50 horses'. When Pease saw an early prototype steam engine in action, he knew Stephenson was right.

A new Act of Parliament was sought that would allow the use of 'loco-motive or moveable engines', which caused some concern among the uninitiated. It also permitted the transport of passengers, although no one believed that would be anything other than a distraction from the real business of hauling coal.

NEXT ON THE LINE CAME DARLINGTON, IN NORTH YORKSHIRE, A PLACE OF PILGRIMAGE FOR RAILWAY HISTORIANS

Although it was expensive, steam traction was reliable, and the idea attracted interest from numerous investors. At first the Stockton & Darlington Railway was open to anyone who paid to use the line. It meant trains ran on a whim on the same tracks used by horse-drawn loads. Fights often broke out when rival operators argued over rights of way. In 1833 horses and rival operators were evicted when the S&DR became sole operator. Parallel tracks were laid so trains could travel in opposite directions, and a signalling system of sorts was installed.

Its smooth running became a model for other railways to mimic. Among the early companies to follow suit was the Whitby & Pickering Railway, which began in 1836. It was to Whitby, over to the east on the Yorkshire coast, that our journey took us next.

Whitby was once an important port – in 1828 it ranked seventh in England. It was here that Captain James Cook (1728–79) was born, and it was in a former Whitby collier, the *Endeavour*, that he explored Australia and the South Seas. Bradshaw clearly liked it in Whitby, writing: 'There are, among the watering places of England, few that have been more greatly benefited than Whitby from railway communication or that have become better adapted for the reception of visitors.'

For Bradshaw roles are reversed in Whitby. Here, instead of him quoting others, it is his book that is mentioned in Bram Stoker's *Dracula*, albeit years after his death. 'Dracula consults his Bradshaw guide before the 9.30 goods train to King's Cross from Whitby station, in one of his 50 coffins ...'

As well as the station, there are numerous other Dracula-linked landmarks to spot in Whitby, including Dracula's Seat, with its stunning view across Whitby Bay, the Tate Sands, where Dracula jumped from ship to shore as a black dog, and the Royal Hotel, where Dracula spent his first night in England.

Author Bram Stoker (1847–1912) visited Whitby during a career spent writing, reviewing and acting as agent for actor Henry Irving. It's said he was told a grisly tale about a shipwreck which took place some years previously and resulted in a cargo of coffins being loosed into the sea. The following day, apparently, horrified Whitby folk were confronted with the sight of decomposing bodies scattered along the beach. The drama of the east Yorkshire coast combined with Stoker's fertile imagination to create the rest of a story which was published in 1897 but remained relatively unknown until it attracted the attention of early Hollywood film-makers.

BEYOND SHEER HEIGHTS AND GOTHIC HORROR, WHITBY IS ALSO KNOWN FOR A GEMSTONE

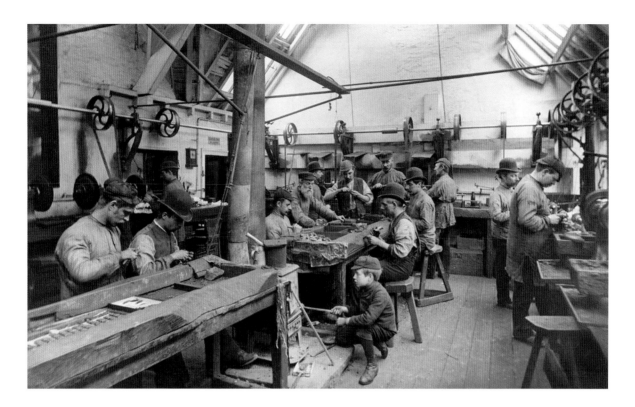

Stoker clearly shared Bradshaw's affection for the ancient town with its romantic abbey ruins. According to Bradshaw, 'Whitby has long been admired for the peculiarity of its position and the grandeur of its coast scenery. To the eastward the cliffs rise abruptly, nearly 200 ft above the sea, and towards the south present a succession of bold headlands. To the north the views along the coast are not less imposing.'

Beyond sheer heights and Gothic horror, Whitby is also known for a gemstone which was immensely popular in Victorian times. Jet is one of two British gemstones and it is found only in a seven-mile stretch of coastline around Whitby. It comes from fossilised monkey puzzle trees.

Jet came into fashion after the death of Prince Albert in 1861, after which Queen Victoria would only countenance the wearing of black jewellery at court. Jet became so popular that there were more than 200 workshops spread throughout Whitby in the 1870s, with a combined turnover of £3 million. One firm alone employed 1,700 people. Craftsmen from all over Europe arrived to cash in on the trend for coal-coloured artefacts. The largest piece of jet ever found in Whitby is about 12 feet long.

ABOVE: **JET WORKSHOPS WERE BIG BUSINESS DURING VICTORIAN TIMES IN WHITBY, WHERE THE GEMSTONE IS FOUND.**

OVERLEAF: **MYSTERIOUS WHITBY FAMOUSLY FEATURED IN BRAM STOKER'S 1897 NOVEL, DRACULA.**

From Whitby we turned back inland and travelled past the Cleveland Hills on our way to Harrogate which, like Whitby, has retained much of its Victorian flavour.

Another Victorian trend emerges at Harrogate, for it was here that the first Turkish bath in Britain was built – and it's still in marvellous order. A Turkish bath usually has three rooms, each with air heated to different temperatures, and a plunge pool. It was opened to the public at a time when cleanliness was not high on many people's agenda.

The man usually credited with bringing the Turkish bath to Britain is David Urquhart (1805–77), a Scottish diplomat, MP for Stafford and public opponent of Russia's political ambitions, including its threat to the Ottoman Empire. To counter this, Urquhart sought to popularise Turkish culture. He was briefly secretary at the British consulate in Constantinople (now Istanbul), and he describes the baths he saw there in his book *The Pillars of Hercules*, published in 1850. They were the kind of baths the Romans would recognise.

Having suffered periods of ill health which were alleviated by different forms of hydrotherapy, Urquhart was in no doubt that people would benefit from use of the baths. There was, he said, 'a chapter [in his book] which, if the reader will peruse it with diligence and apply with care, may prolong his life, fortify his body, diminish his ailments, augment his enjoyments, and improve his temper: then having found something beneficial to himself, he may be prompted to do something to secure the like for his fellow-creatures.'

It was his firm belief that baths like this should be freely available to the public. Victorians embraced the principle of Turkish baths, but many built during the era closed down in the twentieth century and of those that remain several are at risk of closure.

Our journey through northern Britain then took us to the forerunner of today's recycling businesses at Batley, between Leeds and Huddersfield in West Yorkshire.

Benjamin Law (1773–1837) first began using discarded wool for blankets, coats, carpets and fertiliser back in 1813. He blended it with new wool at a time when the Napoleonic Wars had left the country short of raw materials. Before long, wool waste was being brought to Batley from all over the world to be ground up into a gritty, fibrous dust known as 'shoddy'. Shoddy was particularly sought after for the making of military uniforms. Later Law's nephews worked out how to incorporate tailor's

clippings, and the by-product was called 'mungo'. By 1860 Batley was producing around 7,000 tons of shoddy and mungo per year.

Batley's railway station, which opened in 1848, serving the main line to Leeds and Huddersfield and several branch lines, was ideally suited to this industry, as in those days it had eight platforms upon which wool and textiles could be off-loaded.

Law's contribution to the local economy is recalled on his gravestone, which reads: '[his] invention of shoddy converted Batley from an industrial village into a busy manufacturing town'. And in the Yorkshire tradition of 'waste not, want not' the mills that once produced material across the region are now themselves being recycled, into offices and shopping centres.

Another commercial interest that boomed with the railways is the rhubarb-growing industry at nearby Woodlesford, south-east of Leeds on the River Aire. The railway reached here in 1840 as trains forged through on the North Midland Line between Derby and Leeds. Rhubarb crops were loaded on for distribution across the country.

After Woodlesford became an unmanned halt in 1970 the station was demolished. By then the 'rhubarb specials' that once took the morning crop down the line, destination London, were already a distant memory. When production was at its peak before 1939, incredibly, 200 tons of rhubarb would be carried daily on the railways.

Rhubarb was grown in heated sheds in the dark, 'forcing' an early and tender crop. A business that started in 1877, it used shoddy as fertiliser and coal to heat the growing sheds, and both were transported there by train. But the nation's love for rhubarb declined with the introduction of an increasing variety of succulent foreign fruits. Only a handful of farms remain in business.

Our journey then took us through the coal-mining areas of Wakefield and Barnsley and on to the southern tip of Yorkshire and to Sheffield. Strangely, this vibrant city appears to have once been unusually class-ridden. One of the first things we learnt on arrival was that when the station was built in 1845 it had separate entrances for different classes of traveller.

Recognised by Bradshaw as the 'great seat of the cutlery trade', Sheffield had been famous for cutlery making since the fourteenth century. Following the invention of the steel-making process in the eighteenth century, Sheffield became Britain's steel capital – and soon

it wasn't just cutlery. Bradshaw lists the products that emerged from
Sheffield in Victorian times. 'Knives, forks, razors, Britannia metal,
Sheffield plate, scythes, garden implements, files, screws, other tools,
stoves, fenders as well as engines, railway springs and buffers – steel
being the basis of nearly all.'

On the strength of its steel industry, at the beginning of the twentieth
century Sheffield was the world's tenth largest city. 'Made in Sheffield'
was seen on cutlery used all over the world and, in the arms race that
preceded the First World War, the armour plating for Britain's new
Dreadnoughts was mostly made in Sheffield.

From Sheffield it's a short train journey south to Nottingham, whose
main product could not be more different. What Sheffield was for steel,
Nottingham was for stockings and lace. For centuries 'the Queen of
the Midlands' had been a hosiery town, and in 1589 a local man, the
Rev. William Lee, invented the stocking-frame, which enabled stockings to be made far more quickly than they could be knitted by hand.
Even so it remained a cottage industry, until the Industrial Revolution.

Bradshaw said of Nottingham, 'Silk, cotton stockings and bobbin-net
lace are the staple manufactures. Until recently the bobbins were usually worked upon frames rented from the employers but this to a great
extent has been altered since the introduction of the round frames,
which are now generally confined to factories.'

With the Industrial Revolution came the power-loom and the flying
shuttle, and crafts like weaving and lace-making moved into factories,
to be done mechanically. The stocking-frame was also adapted, so that
lace-making too was mechanised. It was now that Nottingham came to
be closely associated with cotton-spinning.

The move into factories meant low pay and terrible conditions for
working people, whose resentment ultimately boiled over. Nottingham
became the birthplace of the movement that tried to stop the Industrial
Revolution in its tracks.

In 1811, while Britain was still suffering the privations caused by
the Napoleonic Wars, a radical group known as the Luddites was
formed. Taking their name from the probably fictional Ned Ludd, or
King Ludd, they set out to destroy the technology that they believed
was threatening their livelihoods. Groups of men burst into factories and smashed up the machinery, in particular the 'wide frames',
which could make stockings in large quantities and far more cheaply

WHAT SHEFFIELD WAS FOR STEEL, NOTTINGHAM WAS FOR STOCKINGS AND LACE

than could a skilled craftsman. The Luddite movement spread from Nottingham throughout the north, attracting such enormous levels of support that the army was at times called in to quell unrest. Frustrated by this secretive but effective army of the poor, the government resorted to making machine breaking a capital offence, and men were consequently hanged or transported for Luddite activity. By 1817, as the wealth of the nation improved, the movement had died out.

From Nottingham we headed south-east on the last leg of the journey. The end of the line is Melton Mowbray in Leicestershire, a town solidly rural and traditional in character. Bradshaw described Melton Mowbray as 'the centre of a famous hunting country. Horses are bred here; its pork pies and Stilton cheese are also valuable productions.' Today Melton Mowbray remains the headquarters of hunting, the Quorn, Cottesmore and Belvoir all hunting in the vicinity, while the cheese made there includes both Stilton and Red Leicester.

Stilton cheese is a delicacy made only in Leicestershire, Nottinghamshire and Derbyshire, and has European Union Protected Designation of Origin status, like Parma ham. It means that cheese made anywhere else can't be called Stilton. The local cheese industry had a notable spin-off. The excess whey from cheese production led to the keeping of pigs on a large scale – and the development of the pork pie industry.

There is also a link between pork pies and hunting. Pigs were slaughtered in the autumn and winter, the hunting seasons. And the pies that were produced afterwards were popular with the hunt servant, who would pop one into his pocket before trekking around the countryside in the wake of the hunt. The tasty snacks soon came to the notice of the huntsmen, who began taking pork pies of their own.

As early as 1831 the Leeds to London stagecoach was being used to take Melton Mowbray pork pies to London for sale. The arrival of the railways took production to another level, with new bakehouses springing up close to the station. With the age of refrigeration, the brand went global.

It's another example of how railway innovation boosted everyday business in city, town and village. Since the railway's inception, some associated trades have come and gone. Others, like the humble pork pie, have been robust enough to stand the test of time.

CRK

HIRE

Wyrardisbury

Horton

Perry Oaks

Barracks

Stanwell Moor

Stanwell

West Bedfont

Hatton

Drilling Ground

East Bedfont

FELTHAM STATION

Runny Mead

LONDON & WINDSOR Ry.

17

STAINES

WINDSOR & STH. WEST. RAILWAY

STA

Feltham

Egham

16

Hanworth

Ashford

Penton Hook

Littleton

Charlton

Thorpe

Laleham

Upper Halliford

15

Sunbury

R. Thames

Horton Parks

Hamp

Race C

West Moulsey

Thorpe Gr.

Trottsworth

Obelisk

St Ann's Hill

CHERTSEY

21

Halliford

Walton on Thames

Sandgate

STA

Shepperton

R. Thames

Andrew New Gr.

Oatlands Park

ham Place

Botley's Park

Addlestone

STA

Weybridge 19

Hersham Gr.

Westend

Otter Shaw Park

Otter

River Wey

STATION

Southwood

Br.

Bourn Brook

St Georges Hill

R. Mole

Chobham

Basingstoke Canal

Byfleet

22

Cobham Street

Cobham 26

Woking Heath

Pirford Green

Wisley

Cobham Court

Horsell

JUNCTION STATION

WESTERN Ry.

SOUTH

S

Pirford

U

Hill

Kingsland Gr.

Wey River

Woking 24

Ripley Gr.

Martyrs Gr.

Mays Gr.

Fetcham Common

ded, London Metropolis &c

GODALMING BRANCH

Ripley

Ockham

Eastwick

Send Marsh

Sutton Gr.

Weaham Send

Little Bookham

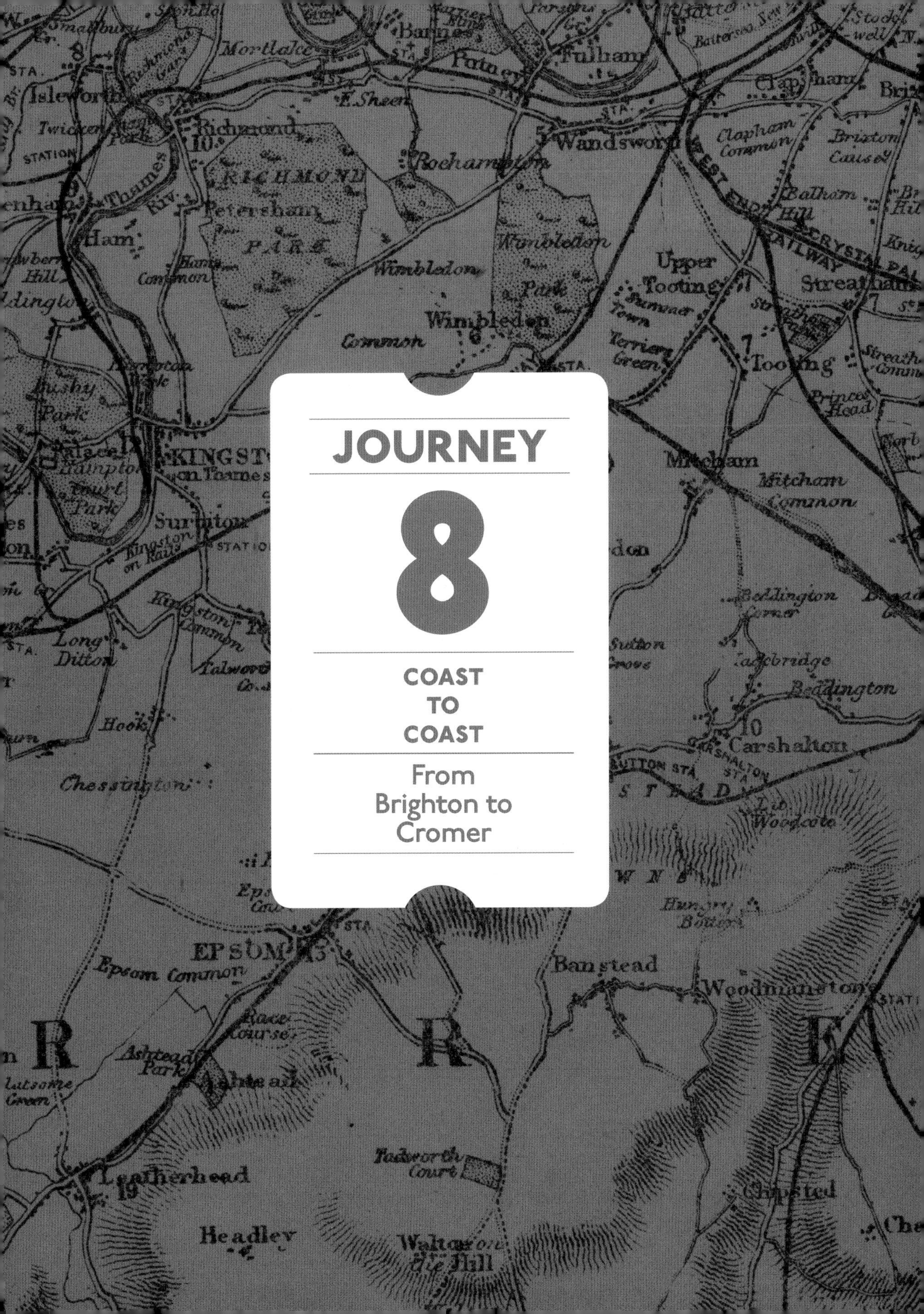

JOURNEY

8

COAST TO COAST

From Brighton to Cromer

Britain's railways were revolutionary. They gave power to ordinary people who at last had a chance to, quite literally, broaden their horizons. Rather than being confined to a single neighbourhood people could visit, or even move to and commute from, coast and countryside. This was especially true of the new middle classes, created by the Industrial Revolution.

For example, the line between Brighton and London was mostly used by passenger trains transporting commuters, shoppers, workers and sports enthusiasts. As technology improved, the journey times were slashed, enticing still more people on to the train. In Bradshaw's day the journey took one and a half hours. By 1865 that had reduced to 75 minutes and today it can be close to 50 minutes.

Bradshaw was acutely aware of the changes afoot. 'Merchants who formerly made Dulwich or Dalston the boundaries of their suburban residences now have got their mansion on the south coast, and still get in less time, by a less expensive conveyance, to their counting houses in the city.'

There was a flipside to the railways that led to financial ruin for many. Although most of these stories are in the shadow of history, this route shines a light on a few.

Brighton was in many ways defined by the Royal Pavilion, a former farmhouse refashioned in 1822 by John Nash (1752–1835), the designer of London's Regent Street. He was acting at the behest of the future George IV (1762–1830), whose patronage made Brighton popular. He first rented the farmouse, in 1783, then bought it and had it transformed.

The Pavilion's onion domes and exotic spires were a nod to India, a country whose importance in terms of trade was escalating. Inside it was sumptuous, a measure of George's extraordinary self-indulgence that ultimately led him into ill health and terrible debt. The planned gardens which were to be in similarly elaborate style were never built.

On the face of it George came to Brighton to take advantage of the benefits of sea bathing, made popular after 1750 by prescription of local doctor Richard Russell. In fact, he was shadowing his mistress Maria Fitzherbert, who had a house there. Fitzherbert was a Catholic, so marriage was out of the question for the heir to the British throne. He later married Caroline of Brunswick and they honeymooned in Brighton. But he so loathed her that she was barred from his coronation in 1821 and afterwards the marriage was dissolved by Parliament.

BRIGHTON'S ROYAL
PAVILION, GEORGE IV'S
FOLLY, IS OVERPOWERINGLY
OSTENTATIOUS, ALTHOUGH IT
HELPED TO CHANGE THE TOWN'S
FORTUNES FOR THE BETTER.

George's death in 1830 came on the cusp of the railway revolution. Within 20 years the trains transformed Brighton from a royal playground to a busy resort. Queen Victoria had no love for the place or the Pavilion, and in 1850 she sold the bloated palace to Brighton's municipal authority for a fraction of its cost. Later, during the First World War, it was used as a military hospital. Hundreds of Indian soldiers who had been wounded on the Western Front were brought there. It was hoped that the décor and ambience would make them feel at home and aid their recovery.

Bradshaw seems to have shared Queen Victoria's view of the building. 'The Pavilion which rises with domes and minarets, and is fretted with greater variety than taste … erected for George IV after a fanciful oriental model, which, despite its supposed resemblance to the Moscow Kremlin, has had no precedent before or since.'

With his description of the Brighton sea-front he also gives us a few more clues about why Queen Victoria so disliked the town, referring to 'scores of laughing, chubby, thoughtless children, skilled manifestly in the

BELOW: THE WEST PIER WAS CONSIDERED THE MOST ATTRACTIVE OF BRIGHTON'S THREE PIERS UNTIL IT WAS DESTROYED BY FIRE.

OVERLEAF: CRYSTAL PALACE WAS A TRIUMPH OF VICTORIAN ENGINEERING, FIRST SITED IN LONDON'S HYDE PARK AND LATER RELOCATED TO SYDENHAM, WHERE IT STOOD FOR 80 YEARS BEFORE BEING WRECKED IN A BLAZE.

art of ingeniously tormenting maids, tutors, governesses, and mammas; prawn sellers and shellfish hawkers a few, and flymen a multitude, all idly vociferating, whilst intent upon their customary constitutional walk, the morning habitués of the promenade swing lustily past. Let us mingle with the throng and obtain a closer intimacy with the principal features of the place … for amusements, there is no provincial town in the kingdom that can offer such a variety of assembly and concert-rooms, libraries, bazaars, and other expedients for slaughtering our common enemy – time.'

Clearly the train link opened in 1841 had brought an influx of 'commoners' to Brighton. Nor was its arrival entirely good news for commerce in the town. Until the advent of the train Brighton was an essential staging post on the quickest route between London and Paris. Ferries pulled alongside the chain pier, which had been built in 1823 and looked like a stunted suspension bridge, to transport people to Dieppe on the other side of the Channel and onward to the French capital.

When the railway reached nearby Newhaven in 1847, however, its deep-water port was immediately a better option for cross-channel ferries. The chain pier was then used for leisure purposes. As the science of pier building improved, Brighton got not one but two more piers to the west, although only a lone example, the Palace Pier, remains open today. The chain pier was washed away by a storm in 1896, and the West Pier, designed by Victorian architect Eugenius Birch (1816–84) and acclaimed as the most magnificent, was left a skeleton after an arson attack and later succumbed to wind and fire.

Brighton also boasts the oldest aquarium and, along the sea-front, the longest serving electric railway in the world, the brainchild of Magnus Volks (1851–1937). Opened in 1883, it was the first electric railway in the world for public use. For a few years around the turn of the century the line was linked to another Volks creation, the Seashore Railway, which ran all the way from Brighton to Rottingdean on rails built under the sea. Passengers travelled in a tramcar perched on high stilts, which led to the railway being known as 'Daddy Long Legs'. Sadly the Seashore Railway closed in 1901 to make way for sea defences.

Volks also installed electricity in his Brighton house in 1880 and later built an electric car. The Grand Hotel was built in 1864. All these and more are indicators of the lively, outward-looking and affluent resort that Brighton became in the last half of the nineteenth century. The aquarium and sea-front railway are still operational.

PASSENGERS TRAVELLED IN A TRAMCAR PERCHED ON HIGH STILTS, WHICH LED TO THE RAILWAY BEING KNOWN AS 'DADDY LONG LEGS'

On its way from Brighton the London train climbs a valley and then tunnels through the South Downs before continuing north to Haywards Heath and Crawley. When the railway arrived, each of these towns was already well established, with a long history, but elsewhere the line brought sudden changes in status.

Southern Britain was rapidly criss-crossed with railway lines, making small towns out of villages and major commercial centres out of small towns. Two places on the London to Brighton line fall into this category. Gatwick was barely a village when the aerodrome opened in 1936, but since its modernisation and expansion in the 1950s it has been one of Britain's main airports and now has 30 million visitors a year flying to 200 world-wide destinations from its single runway. Further north the line bypassed hilly Reigate, and where it crossed the Guildford to Tonbridge line nearby, the town of Redhill grew so fast that it soon rivalled its senior neighbour in size and commercial importance.

Six miles east of Redhill on the line towards Tonbridge and Ashford is Godstone, where firestone was once quarried. It was used for buildings, in furnaces and as a bed in glass-making. As the 'good stone' quarried here had no grain, it could be cut in any direction. Once the quarry enjoyed a monopoly, but it was killed off in about 1860 by a revolution in transport which led to the arrival of cheaper stone from elsewhere. The quarry caves still contain the original tram lines that brought loaded wagons to the surface. In fact the lines have an older history than that. Before being installed underground they were part of the Croydon, Merstham & Godstone Iron Railway, a horse-drawn tramway that operated between 1803 and 1838, and was then supplanted by the railway.

Continuing north from Redhill, the railway eventually takes us into south London and through Croydon to Sydenham. Here we reach the site of the Crystal Palace, an elegant glass citadel that symbolised the shining hopes and aspirations of the Victorian age.

An immense glazed building, designed by Sir Joseph Paxton (1801–65), was constructed in Hyde Park at the bidding of Prince Albert in 1851 for the Great Exhibition, showcasing Britain's contribution to the Industrial Revolution and cutting-edge technology from the rest of the world. Its construction was made possible by the removal of a tax on glass and the advances in glass manufacturing techniques that followed.

But the Hyde Park exhibition was temporary. In 1854 the magnificent structure was dismantled and reconstructed across London in another

park at Sydenham. Seeking to enhance its reputation, the London, Brighton & South Coast Railway paid for the move, confident that it would recoup costs as passengers used the trains to flock there.

The building remained an exhibition centre and was also used for plays and concerts. The public loved it. Even Bradshaw seems uncharacteristically poetic… 'But when the train approaches the spot where the brilliant and fairy fabric, in the midst of the most enchanting scenery, is revealed suddenly to the eye, the impression produced solicits our warmest admiration … the view of which we may envy the Brighton Railway traveller who enjoys the sight daily in virtue of his season ticket.' It was, the guide insists, 'the most wonderful work human hands and mind have yet achieved'.

The hunch by the rail company about increased passenger numbers paid off, but it couldn't then raise the capital to extend railway lines.

ABOVE: **PREHISTORY WAS A NEW SCIENCE FOR THE VICTORIANS. THE CREATURES CONSTRUCTED AT CRYSTAL PALACE WERE INTERPRETATIONS OF RECENTLY UNEARTHED SKELETONS.**

OVERLEAF: **BURLINGTON ARCADE OPENED IN 1819, OFFERING LONDON SHOPPERS LUXURY, CHOICE AND SECURITY.**

Instead it encouraged the West End of London & Crystal Palace Railway to build a branch line from its station in Sydenham to Crystal Palace itself.

More than 112,000 people visited Crystal Palace by train in a single day in 1859. Inside there were 13,000 exhibits in a building that measured 1,858 feet in length. The square footage inside the glass walls was six times that of St Paul's Cathedral.

Next to the palace were grounds almost as large as Hyde Park, among which were dotted one of its most popular features, life-size models of dinosaurs. This was an early attempt to reconstruct a species recognised by scientists through skeletal excavation in an age when the Bible's version of creation held sway. Created by Professor Richard Owen, the 33 models were built from brick and artificial stone on a framework of iron. Not entirely accurate in their interpretation, they were modelled on partial skeletons that had been discovered and nonetheless pre-dated Charles Darwin's 1859 book *On the Origin of Species* by several years. They represented a bold effort at understanding a distant history with no precedent to follow.

As time went on the popularity of the palace inevitably waned. The 1911 Festival of Empire marked the last of its glory days. The event was swiftly followed by its bankruptcy, and the Crystal Palace was ultimately bought for the nation, to be used as a naval training establishment during the First World War. Finally, disaster struck in 1936 when a small office fire was fanned by the wind into an all-consuming blaze. The Crystal Palace was destroyed by night in a conflagration that could be seen from eight counties.

The park remains, and on and around an island in the lake children can still find excitement in the one feature of the Crystal Palace that's not extinct – the dinosaurs.

Trains from Brighton to London terminate at London Bridge or Victoria, while you can also change at Clapham Junction and arrive at Waterloo. Thanks to the underground services all London stations are highly accessible. Waterloo station was opened in 1848 by the London & South Western Railway, not as a terminal but a stop on a through line. It grew into a jumble of stations, platforms and services until a major refurbishment took place in the first decade of the twentieth century. Among the trains that departed from Waterloo before and after the rebuild was the 'stiffs express', as it was known among railway workers. It was a service run especially for the dead, heading from London to Brookwood Cemetery in Surrey.

The London Necropolis Company, which ran it, was set up in 1850 when the sudden growth in building throughout the capital meant that land for burial was in short supply. The company hit on the idea of ferrying coffins to an out-of-city cemetery where there was plenty of space and which family and friends knew would not be ploughed up by developers within a few years. They found a suitable site at Brookwood, between Woking and Farnborough. When it opened in 1854, the 2,000-acre cemetery was the largest in the world.

At Waterloo a special station was built, designed by Sir William Tite, easily accessible from the company's building in Westminster Bridge Road. Every day an express train departed for Brookwood, bearing coffins and associated mourners, for whom there were three classes of ticket. At Brookwood the cemetery had its own branch line from Necropolis Junction and two stations, one for the Anglican section and one for the Nonconformists. As time went by, the odd golfer was found among the grieving, taking advantage of the service to reach the nearby West Hill Golf Club.

While the cemetery remains, the London Necropolis Company was largely erased in the Second World War, except for the frontage of its administrative offices in the Westminster Bridge Road.

Commuters apart, people using stations in Bradshaw's day were more likely to be shoppers than mourners, because the railways allowed ordinary people easy access of the city. They could refer to Bradshaw's guide, which had plenty of recommendations, including the stylish Burlington Arcade off Piccadilly next to the Royal Academy. 'The visitor should not omit to visit the Burlington arcade, the prettiest gallery in London. It is a facsimile of a portion of the Palais Royal, but the tradesmen who occupy these shops are of a less wealthy class and the place is considered as the fashionable gentleman's lounge.'

It is indeed as elegant as the French palace and, although not as large, it is certainly extremely long. The forerunner of the modern shopping mall, Burlington Arcade was conceived by Lord George Cavendish, ostensibly to make the shopping experience more pleasurable for his wife. Designer Samuel Ware envisaged 'a Piazza for all Hardware, Wearing Apparel and Articles not Offensive in appearance nor smell'.

Since its opening in 1819 the Arcade has been patrolled by Beadles, liveried officers in frock-coats and braided top hats. These were initially drawn from Lord Cavendish's own regiment, the 10th Hussars, to enhance the safety of shoppers. They did so by enforcing the Arcade code, which meant no whistling, singing, playing of musical instruments, running, carrying of large parcels, opening of umbrellas or pushing of prams. Today four beadles continue to uphold the traditional values of Burlington Arcade. As a private police force, which incidentally pre-dates the Metropolitan Police, they have full authority to eject shoppers who fail to comply.

The choice of shopping venues in London now is colossal, and the best way to visit them is by travelling on the underground. On 30 July 1900, the Central London Railway – now called the Central Line –

THE ARMAMENTS FACTORY AT ENFIELD ESTABLISHED IN 1816 WAS OPEN TO ANYONE WHO SECURED A GOVERNMENT ORDER PERMITTING A VISIT.

opened between Bank and Shepherd's Bush. It was nicknamed the 'twopenny tube' for its flat fare and tunnels, and 'the tube' came to be applied to all undergrounds.

The maze of underground tunnels underfoot has often inhibited development in London. However, it didn't prevent the installation of a splendid Masonic temple within the Great Eastern Hotel, which had been built in 1884 near Liverpool Street station as a railway hotel. The lavish Grecian temple was added in 1912 and featured 12 different types of marble and a mahogany throne. Its cost was a cool £50,000, equivalent to about £4 million today, but it had been sealed off until builders discovered it behind a false wall in 1997.

One of the routes that radiate out of London is the line from Liverpool Street towards Harlow and Stansted. About half-way to Harlow, close to the station of Enfield Lock and the River Lea Navigation, is the site of the Royal Small Arms Factory. A housing estate now stands in its place, but this was once the most eminent gun manufacturer in the world. It was so famous that it became something of a tourist attraction. Bradshaw notes: 'The environs of Enfield are exceedingly pretty and the scenery quite picturesque. A visit should be made to the Government Arms factory, an order for which must be previously obtained from the ordenance [sic] office, London.'

The first arms factory was established at Enfield in 1816 by a government concerned at the price and quality of weapons on the open market. The nearby canal solved the problem of water supply needed for steam engines. Every element of the guns was made by hand. The original factory was substantially enlarged in 1854 in response to the Crimean War. It was then that American engineering techniques for mass production, first seen in Britain at the Great Exhibition, were installed.

In time it became more than a factory, as shops, housing, a school and other facilities grew up around it. The station at Enfield Lock opened in 1855, when it was called Ordnance Factory. In 1860 a workforce of 1,000 was producing on average 1,744 rifles every week. By 1887 the workforce had increased by 140 per cent to cope with demand. After learning a trade at the small arms factory apprentices could reasonably hope to get a job anywhere, because their experience was so highly valued.

Guns produced there took the name Enfield or its first two letters – En. Thus the most famous of its products today are probably the Lee-Enfield

A HOUSING ESTATE NOW STANDS IN ITS PLACE, BUT THIS WAS ONCE THE MOST EMINENT GUN MANUFACTURER IN THE WORLD

rifle, Bren light machine-guns and Sten submachine-guns. Its guns have played a part in every major war or armed skirmish that Britain has taken part in during the past 200 years.

Our route continued around the edge of Essex, through Bishop's Stortford and Saffron Walden towards Newmarket. We were heading into some of England's flattest landscapes, so perhaps it's no surprise that Newmarket became the beating heart of horse racing. However, although it was the first venue for regular horse racing, a prejudice against middle-class visitors arriving by rail nearly caused the town to be sidelined.

Until the age of rail travel Newmarket was accustomed to having only aristocrats as race-goers. The influential Jockey Club, which is still based there, assumed that its future lay with society's elite. When the Great Eastern Railway scheduled excursion trains to a station near Newmarket, the Jockey Club's response was to arrange races with a start and finish so far apart that only the monied few who could accompany the riders on horseback or in carriages would watch.

However, rival race tracks were keen to seize the initiative offered by the railways. Horses were transported for miles to make races more competitive. Spectators were welcomed by the hundred. Soon Newmarket found itself on the back foot as owners sought to race at courses most conveniently reached by train. By 1847 the Jockey Club was actively supporting plans for a rail link to its track. Afterwards 'race specials', often double the length of a normal train, were laid on to Newmarket from numerous major cities. Train-travelling politicians were in the habit of attending big races – then racing back to the Houses of Parliament for an evening debate.

On the main line from London and on similarly flat ground lies Cambridge, crowned by its university buildings. 'The University of Cambridge is second to no other in Europe,' states Bradshaw. 'On approaching the town, whether by rail or otherwise, the first object that meets the eye is the Chapel of King's College.'

Although the railway penetrated Cambridge in 1845, the station was built some distance from the city. Rumour had it that this was to make it harder for male students to jump on the train for assignations in London. That may be speculation, but it is true that university dons retained the right to search the station for undergraduates and had an Act of Parliament passed so they could ask railway companies to ban students from travelling even if they had a valid ticket. Nor would the university

UNTIL THE AGE OF RAIL TRAVEL NEWMARKET WAS ACCUSTOMED TO HAVING ONLY ARISTOCRATS AS RACE-GOERS

countenance trains running on a Sunday through Cambridge station. This rule stayed in place until 1908.

However, the authorities at Cambridge were more forward-thinking when it came to football. Records show that in the sixteenth century football or something like it was being played at Cambridge, and in the nineteenth century it was the public school sport of choice. However, there was scant regard for an opponent's well-being as players used hands as well as feet, and body checks, kicking and tripping to win. What's more, each team played according to its own set of rules.

In 1848 a meeting of University players was held in Cambridge which resulted in a definitive set of rules being agreed. Copies were pinned to the trees surrounding Parker's Piece, the park in the middle of Cambridge which was a favourite spot for games. Although not universally accepted, the Cambridge rules did help to impose some order on an otherwise unruly and often violent game. (Games between 'town' and 'gown' were particu-

CAMBRIDGE UNIVERSITY'S FOOTBALL CLUB WAS ONE OF THE FIRST TO ADOPT NEW RULES THAT TOOK HAND BALLS, BODY CHECKS AND HIGH KICKS OUT OF THE GAME.

ELY
IT'S QUICKER BY RAIL
ILLUSTRATED BOOKLET FREE FROM L·N·E·R OFFICES AND AGENCIES
OR INFORMATION BUREAU, I MINSTER PLACE, ELY, CAMBRIDGESHIRE

JARROLD & SONS, LTD. NORWICH & LONDON   Printed in Great Britain   1940   Published by the LONDON & NORTH EASTERN RAILWAY

larly feisty affairs.) They became the foundation of the rules drawn up in 1863 by the newly founded Football Association.

Railways also played a part in popularising the game, by taking teams across the country for matches and supporters to games.

As the line heads further into the Fens the land is not only flat but low-lying. The Norman founders of the immense Ely cathedral sited it on the highest piece land in the region, and its vast tower with its magnificent octagonal lantern can be seen from many miles away. The surrounding land was at best marshy, at worst underwater, and in the seventeenth century the first attempts at reclamation began. In 1670 Dutchman Cornelius Vermuyden constructed enormous drains that wiped out parts of the traditional wetlands.

The drainage was not entirely successful, and wind-powered pumps were installed to finish the job. Once drained of water, however, the peaty bottom of the fens shrank and the fields became lower still. After rivers burst their banks the fens were underwater once more. Only when coal-powered steam engines were introduced did man finally overcome nature. According to Bradshaw, 'The productive and remunerative farming of the Fens of Norfolk is one of the greatest triumphs of steam, for that was the effective agent employed to give value to, or rather to create, this extensive territory. Even within a recent period land estimated at £3 or £4 an acre has been enhanced in value, not only one hundred percent but even one hundred fold.'

As sluices were built to back high tides and help drain excess rainfall, more of the Fens were conquered. The land turned over to agriculture was so productive that the region has become known as the breadbasket of England.

The station at King's Lynn on the Norfolk coast is the terminus of the Fen Line from Cambridge. King's Lynn was one of the few towns to feel the pinch when the railway turned up in the town in 1846. The once bustling port went into decline when coal was then transported by rail rather than sea. But the town made a swift recovery as the railway shifted produce and seafood to London and welcomed train-loads of tourists.

King's Lynn sits on The Wash, an extensive area of estuaries, marshes and tidal mud flats. For centuries the ambitious have dreamed of reclaiming land from the sea there. According to Bradshaw, 'Here since 1850 works on a large scale have been carried out for reclaiming part of The Wash but its practicality is doubtful.' Now hopes of extending the

THE LANDMARK CATHEDRAL AT ELY, BUILT IN NORMAN TIMES BY BENEDICTINE MONKS, CAN BE SEEN FOR MILES AND ITS AWESOME SILHOUETTE WAS AN INSPIRATION FOR PILGRIMS.

land at the expense of the sea have come to an end with the realisation that, left untouched, the salt marshes provide a natural buffer to coastal erosion by exhausting the power of the waves. Consequently the area remains as it has always been, and a perfect habitat for wading birds and seals. Our journey then took us east across Norfolk to Norwich, which was linked to the national railway grid in 1845. Already its pre-eminence in the textile industry had been lost, probably because other mill towns had been quicker to join up with the railways.

Norwich maintained a measure of magnificence, though, as Bradshaw reveals. 'The prospect of the city from a little distance is both imposing and beautiful. The massive walls of the old castle crowning the summit of the hill form the central object in view; the lofty spire of the cathedral and those of the numerous parish churches rising in all directions, give it an air of great magnificence and, mixed with this architectural grandeur, is much more than the usual share of rural scenery … many large spaces laid out as gardens or planted with fruit trees.'

Norwich was home to Gurney's Bank, founded in 1770 by a respected Quaker family, the fate of which became inextricably linked with that of the railways. The bank was highly regarded, as Bradshaw confirms. 'On Bank Plain is Gurney's Bank, established by an old Norfolk family, equally known for their good works and philanthropy.' Prisoner reformer Elizabeth Fry (1780–1845) was born into the Gurney family.

Through a subsidiary – Overend, Gurney & Company – the bank was drawn into 'railway mania', which amounted to feverish share buying followed by a financial crash. For, while the railways frequently brought prosperity, investment in some other railway schemes spelled ruin for a number of people and institutions. For this reason the railway companies had a dubious reputation.

There were two bouts of 'railway mania'. The first was in the 1840s when there was a headlong rush to exploit the riches that railways were thought to yield. But lines and locomotives were costly to build. Those that became operational weren't always profitable. People lost money after investing in plans that failed to become reality or companies that couldn't sustain services.

It was a similar story in the 1860s when Overend, Gurney & Company was heavily committed in railway investments. Creditors panicked and rushed to withdraw their savings. The bank went into liquidation in June 1866 owing about £11 million – that's equivalent to about £1 billion today.

THE AREA REMAINS AS IT HAS ALWAYS BEEN, AND A PERFECT HABITAT FOR WADING BIRDS AND SEALS

RIGHT: **COLMAN'S MUSTARD WAS ESTABLISHED IN NORWICH IN 1823 AND MADE HISTORY 55 YEARS LATER BY STARTING CONTRACT FARMING.**

OVERLEAF: **CROMER'S GOLDEN AGE HAS GONE AND ITS FIGHT FOR A SHARE OF THE TOURIST SHILLING IS MADE MORE ARDUOUS BY THE LOSS OF RAIL SERVICES.**

COLMAN'S
MUSTARD
ALL OVER THE WORLD.

NER

Overend, Gurney & Co. were among 200 companies that failed in the crisis. Writer Charles Dickens laid the blame at the door of the overly ambitious railway companies and a government which had allowed them to perpetuate chaos. Happily, Gurney's of Norwich survived and merged with others to form Barclay's Bank in 1896.

Investors might have done better putting their money with another Norwich firm, J. & J. Colman, the mustard makers who have been in business since 1823. Colman's initiated contract farming in 1878, an agreement that meant the farmer was assured of a buyer for his crops while the buyer was certain of supplies for his company.

By the end of the nineteenth century Colman's was such a huge concern that it had its own railway system serving its warehouses and factory, and its own station. The company also provided a school for employees' children from 1857 and a company nurse from 1864. Since 1866, the year it was awarded a Royal Warrant, the mustard has been sold with its hallmark red and yellow packaging.

Due north of Norwich lies the charming coastal town of Cromer. Once a small fishing village, it was not connected with the rest of Britain by rail until 1877, but when it was discovered by Britain's holidaymakers its streets and beaches were soon filled. Most sampled Cromer crab, for which the resort is famous.

Trippers, who could disembark at three stations from destinations across the Midlands and the North, walked on the promenade, which was in fact a massive sea wall installed by the Victorians to fend off coastal erosion. For later generations this has meant major maintenance costs and the growing realisation that defences don't stop erosion but move the problem on to a different section of coast. As the battle against the encroaching sea continues, in areas away from towns authorities have been compelled to take the attitude 'let it be'.

Like Brighton at the start of the journey, Cromer was propelled into the public's affection in the age of the train. Along the way there are numerous examples of how financial disaster followed in the wake of the railways: a bankrupt business here, a squeezed industry there. The trump card played by the railways was always the arrival of visitors. Brighton, which still has a vibrant railway service, continues to prosper. Cromer, where rail services have been cut, must battle harder for its share of the tourist trade.

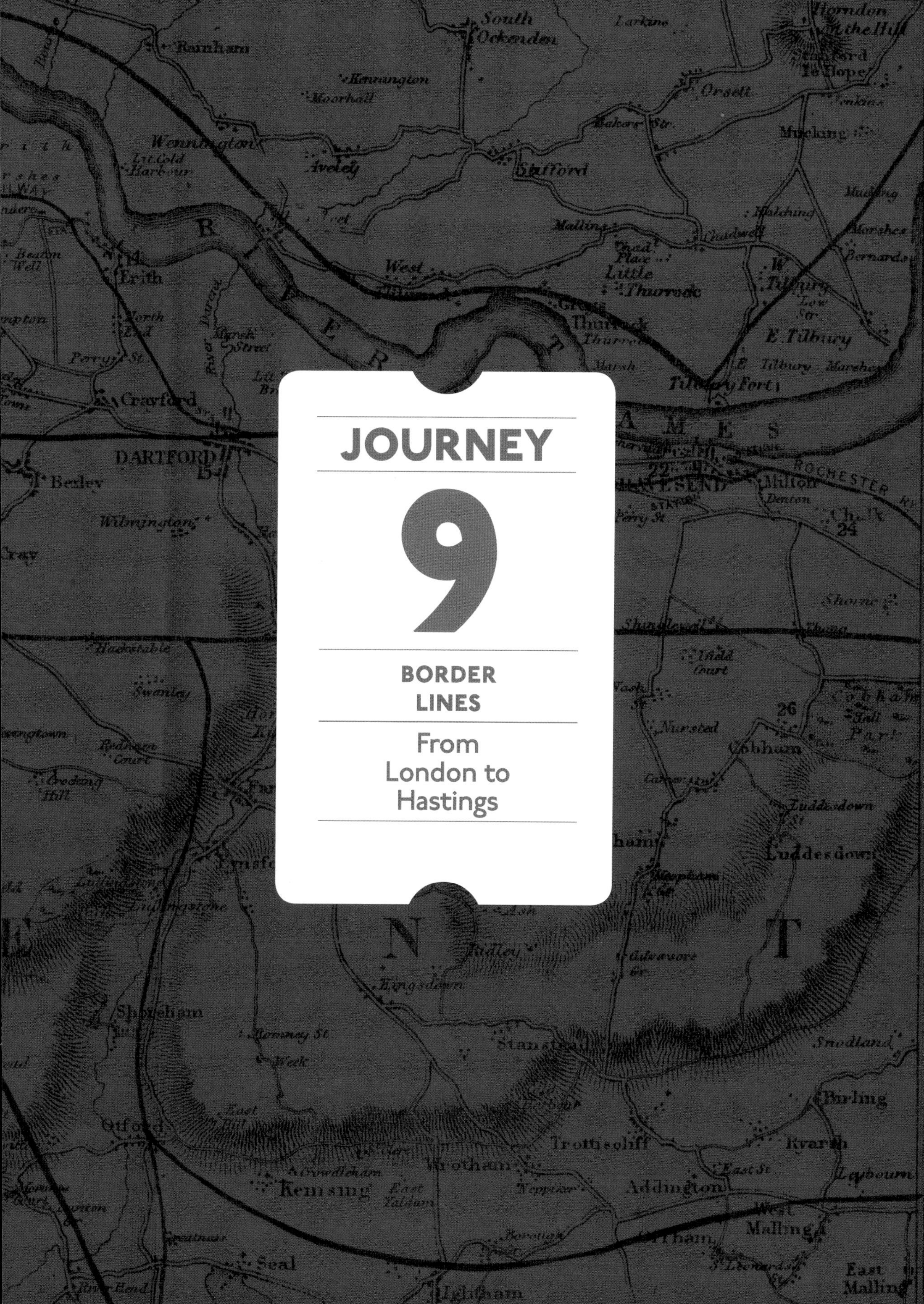

JOURNEY

9

BORDER LINES

From London to Hastings

K ent is a county of contrasts. On the one hand it is like London's allotment, with a history of growing food and fruit aplenty on its fertile fields. Yet throughout history it has also been England's first line of defence. In the nineteenth century, an era when again England's enemies were close by in Europe, it was Kent that was specially fortified to keep them at bay.

There are few ways to better illuminate the light and shade of south-east England than a train journey from London. And any trip heading towards Kent from the capital traditionally began at London Bridge station, which receives fulsome praise from Bradshaw. 'The platforms are spacious and extensive; the wooden roofs over them are light and airy; and the plates of glass diffuse sufficient light to every part of the vast area …'

Those words would be enough to make today's commuters who pass through the station choke on their cappuccinos. It's now dark, over-crowded and quite confusing thanks to a 1970s rebuild. The current multimillion pound redevelopment should see it transformed again into something light and airy.

London Bridge station was the terminal for the city's first railway line heading south-east. Unlike most other railways around the country, this three-and-a-half-mile stretch was built with passengers rather than cargo in mind. The line travelled on viaducts through heavily popu-lated districts, in turn spawning colonies that lived and worked in the 878 railway arches beneath. It opened in 1836, and within 20 years there were 10 million passengers using the line, travelling between London and the suburb of Greenwich.

Not everyone, though, saw the railways as something that would last. A writer in the *Quarterly Review* declared: 'Can anything be more palpably ridiculous than the prospect held out of locomotives travel-ling twice as fast as stage coaches? … we will back Old Father Thames against the Greenwich railway for any sum.'

Three years before it became the terminal on this early railway, Greenwich already had another historic role to play in the history of transport. It became home in 1833 to the influential time ball installed at the Royal Observatory, which had been built on the highest point in Greenwich Park in 1675.

The time ball had been invented by a Royal Navy captain in 1829 and was first in action at Portsmouth Harbour. Its purpose was to give

LONDON BRIDGE STATION, WHICH OPENED FIVE YEARS AFTER THE THAMES BRIDGE, WAS INITIALLY PRAISED FOR BEING SPACIOUS, LIGHT AND AIRY.

passing ships an accurate time, which in turn would help them determine longitude and thus their position.

At Greenwich the distinctive red ball straddles a pole perched on top of the Observatory. Each day at lunchtime the ball is hoisted to the top of the pole and then, at exactly 1 p.m., it is released, falling to the bottom of the pole within easy view of London's shipping. Although midday seems a more significant moment in time, 1 p.m. was traditionally the time when mariners worked out longitude by the position of the sun. Time balls acted like a bridge between sundials and accurate clocks. After radio time signals were introduced in the 1920s they were largely obsolete.

The time ball at Greenwich has particular importance as this location was chosen as the prime meridian of the world in 1884. The prime meridian is the starting point for different time zones. It was an obvious choice because the US had already established its time zones in accordance with Greenwich, as had many of the existing sea charts.

Bradshaw highlights another Greenwich tradition that sadly no longer exists. 'Approaching Greenwich reach, where large quantities of whitebait are caught in the season … Whitebait dinners form the chief attraction to the taverns adjacent, and here Her Majesty's ministers for the time being regale themselves annually on that fish; the season is from May to the latter end of July when parliament generally closes for the season.'

The ministerial whitebait dinners haven't been held since 1894, the last being on August 15 at the invitation of the Prime Minister.

For railway buffs there's a recently opened line in London linking north and south. This addition to the network brought new life to a tunnel built under the Thames by Marc Isambard Brunel, with the help of his son Isambard Kingdom. When it opened in 1843 the Wapping to Rotherhithe tunnel was the first ever built under a river. Its construction was an arduous process which took almost 20 years, during which time a deluge of river water nearly claimed Marc Brunel's life. Following the accident he invented a tunnel shield to protect workers from collapse, and the associated perils of drowning. This device, which kept the exposed face to a minimum and allowed the newly dug section to be shored up, is still used today in underwater tunnelling. Despite that, it was still a dreary task, with sewage from the Thames seeping through the tunnel walls and dangerously compromising workers' health.

THE TIME BALL
AT GREENWICH
HAS PARTICULAR
IMPORTANCE AS
THIS LOCATION
WAS CHOSEN
AS THE PRIME
MERIDIAN OF THE
WORLD IN 1884

The original plan to use the tunnel for carriages was abandoned because money ran out before the approaches could be completed. Nevertheless it was initially a popular attraction as a pedestrian tunnel, housing underground shops and stalls, until it got a reputation for thievery and prostitution. In 1865 it was taken over by the East London Railway Company, who built a railway through it linking existing lines north and south of the river. This was eventually absorbed into the underground system as the East London line, and has recently been revamped as an overground line for London's 2012 Olympics. The history of the tunnel can be studied at a museum in the original engine house at Rotherhithe built to hold the machinery that pumped water out of the tunnel.

To continue our journey into Kent we decided that instead of using the slower Victorian line that still exists, we would take the High Speed Link from St Pancras to Kent, opened in 2007 and the first domestic line of its kind in the country. Michael was transport minister when the plans were initially drawn up. Getting the tunnel off or under the ground was a huge struggle and one of which Michael jokes he still bears the scars.

Chatham and its historic dockyard on the Medway are just 40 minutes from St Pancras station, saving us 20 minutes or more on the London Bridge route.

Ever since Henry VIII set up the dockyard there in the early sixteenth century Chatham has been famous as a place where ships, including Nelson's *Victory*, were built, repaired and maintained. But in the nineteenth century, with the threat from Europe looming, there was a major escalation of scale. The dockyard was made five times its original size and a narrow-gauge railway was installed to move men and equipment around it. There was no doubt in anyone's mind at the time that a strong navy could deter would-be invaders and maintain the British Empire.

Bradshaw was admiring, if not entirely accurate: 'The Dockyard was commenced by Queen Elizabeth,' he states, 'and is about a mile long. It contains six buildings, slips, wet and dry docks. Rope House 1,140 ft long. Blacksmith's shops. Steam saw-mills, oar and block machinery by Brunel.'

Although the dockyard is now open only as a museum, its rope-making facilities are still operational and remain unrivalled. Rope has been made

GETTING THE TUNNEL OFF OR UNDER THE GROUND WAS A HUGE STRUGGLE AND ONE OF WHICH MICHAEL JOKES HE STILL BEARS THE SCARS

RIGHT: CHATHAM DOCKYARD HAS A PROUD HISTORY FROM WHEN THE ROYAL NAVY'S 'WOODEN WALLS' WERE BRITAIN'S BEST DEFENCE, THROUGH TWO WORLD WARS UNTIL ITS CLOSURE.

OVERLEAF: WHILE HOP-PICKING IS NO MORE IN KENT THANKS TO MACHINES, GRAPE-PICKING, HERE AT THE TENTERDEN VINEYARD PARK, IS FIRMLY ON THE AGENDA AS THE COUNTY WINS ACCLAIMS FOR ITS WINES.

on the site since 1618. After 1826 the process was mechanised with steam-powered machines positioned in a rope-walk building that is about a quarter of a mile in length, to accommodate laying the longest rope. Some of the kit from that era is still in use today. However, the rope that's made there now isn't for the Royal Navy but is used for sailing ships. Being made of natural fibres, it's also perfect for zoos, where it is used to help cage animals who try to gnaw to freedom.

To protect Chatham docks a number of brick-lined ditches were built, known as 'the lines'. More than a mile long and reinforced by two square redoubts, they were once the site of mock battles staged by servicemen at Chatham.

A few miles to the south on the old line to Maidstone is the village of Aylesford, which in Bradshaw's day was known entirely for its hop production. Hops were used to preserve and flavour beer. The arrival of the trains in Kent's hop grounds solved a seasonal labour shortage for farmers there, as they carried women and children from London's East End on 'hopping specials'. These city folk would set about the annual harvest, staying in 'hopping huts' and being rewarded with food and some wages. Although they rose at dawn, they got fresh air and exercise, which were widely believed to improve their health and that of the children. The evenings were the most popular time, with dinner, usually cooked on a camp fire, and a sing-song. At weekends extra trains were laid on so that the pickers could be joined by family and friends.

By the twentieth century hop picking attracted some 250,000 men, women and children to Kent at harvest time. Most thought of it as a holiday with pay, but it was not universally popular. Writer George Orwell (1903–50) was unhappy with the wages and conditions and insisted: 'Hop picking is in the category of things that are great fun when they are over.'

After the Second World War machines were brought in to replace labourers, and London's East Enders found other places to holiday. The hop farms that remain in business use their crops for herbal remedies and decoration rather than brewing. It's usually imported hops that go into beers these days.

From Aylesford the line continues into Maidstone, further up the River Medway. When a railway was first proposed for Maidstone there was a barrage of opposition, led by the mayor, who suggested it would be 'ruined as a commercial town'. Consequently the main line to Dover was built six miles to the south of the town. Of course, it was a mam-

moth mistake. Within a few years there was a branch line to Maidstone and it was directly linked to London by rail after 1874. Immediately trains were transporting a new innovation in paper from the mills of Maidstone to some of the highest and most influential houses in the land. James Whatman (1702–59) was a craftsman who developed a more even product called 'wove' paper to replace the rough stuff that had existed before. His son, also called James, introduced further refinements, to make it whiter and smoother than ever.

Wove paper was used by painters J.M.W. Turner and Thomas Gainsborough, poet William Blake, Napoleon, who wrote his will on it, and Queen Victoria. It was even selected for the document recording the peace treaty between the US and Japan that ended the Second World War.

An hour and a train change later we were in the spa town of Tunbridge Wells, in genteel commuter country to the south-west. Along with nearby Tonbridge, it became a centre for the manufacture of leather cricket balls which were then shipped across the country by rail.

The advent of railways changed the face of cricket in other ways too. At the beginning of the nineteenth century cricket was a game for the aristocracy and their staff only. By the end of the century it was open to all, with village and county games played by the most talented rather than the richest men. For the first time teams could travel considerable distances for matches in a matter of hours rather than days.

We continued down a branch line from Ashford – the major railway junction in the region – to Canterbury, not least because Bradshaw waxes lyrical about the trip. '[At Ashford] the line branches off to Canterbury, Whitstable, Sandwich, Deal, Ramsgate and Margate and from the accommodation it affords to the towns through which it passes and the exquisite beauty of the scenery along its route, will not suffer in any comparison with any line of similar length in the kingdom. It follows throughout the meanderings of the River Stour and traversing the most fertile districts in the country, has one uninterrupted panorama of luxuriant fertility … Thence the windings of the Stour, spanned ever and anon by some rustic bridge of wood or stone, enhances the romantic beauty of the landscape and we seem to be for many miles treading the sylvan labyrinth of a miniature Rhine-land.'

At Canterbury Bradshaw was once again bowled over, this time by the numerous medieval features of a city he branded 'exquisitely beautiful'.

Unfortunately, Canterbury was extensively bombed during the Second World War and much of what he saw was turned to dust.

Canterbury was a victim of the raids carried out in April and June 1942 that became known as the Baedeker Blitz. Baedeker was the name of a tourist guide that featured Britain and was available in Germany. Frustrated by Royal Air Force raids on its own historic cities and towns, the Germans pledged to target every British city marked with three stars in the Baedeker guide. Exeter, Norwich, Bath and York were subjected to terrifying raids after the historic ports of Lübeck and Rostock were bombed. Canterbury was attacked after Cologne was substantially

CANTERBURY

FREQUENT TRAINS & CHEAP FARES

SOUTHERN RAILWAY

SOUTHERN RAILWAY ADVERTISING

Printed in England at THE BAYNARD PRESS, LONDON, S.W.9

THE LINE,
ANOTHER GEORGE
AND ROBERT
STEPHENSON
PRODUCTION,
WAS BUILT AS
EARLY AS 1830

destroyed. Both the Luftwaffe and the Royal Air Force were deliberately targeting civilians in undefended cities rather than military targets, in the hope of destroying morale.

It's a lesser known fact that the first railway season tickets were issued at Canterbury in 1834 for people regularly visiting the beach at Whitstable from there during the summer months. The trippers were travelling on the six-mile 'Crab and Winkle' line, so named because it shared the same two first letters as destinations Canterbury and Whitstable, and to underline the fact that the shellfish industry was in full swing at the coast.

The line, another George and Robert Stephenson production, was built as early as 1830 and led to a new harbour being built in Whitstable. It was open several months before the Liverpool & Manchester railway. However, the line involved steep gradients and initially the carriages were pulled by ropes reeled in and out by two stationary, steam-driven winding engines along the route. As such, it's mostly under the radar of the railway record books.

Even today the catch at Whitstable usually includes whelks, the poor man's oyster, which was a staple dish on the bar of London pubs. We met the West family, fourth-generation whelk fishermen, whose great-grandfather came to Whitstable from Norfolk in 1901, bringing with him the innovation of the whelk pot that dramatically improved catches.

Further east down the branch line from Ashford is the resort of Margate, where sea bathing first became popular. Bradshaw clearly gets a measure of the town. 'There is not in the whole range of our seaside physiology a more lively, bustling place than this said Margate; albeit by those who are fettered down to cold formalities and regard laughter as a positive breech of good-breeding, it is pronounced to be essentially and irredeemably vulgar. The streets are always a scene of continued excitement, and troops of roguish ruddy cheeked urchins escorted by their mammas traverse every thoroughfare …

'In short for those who do not go to the coast for retirement and who like to have an atmosphere of London life surrounding them at the seaside there is no place where their desires can be so easily and comprehensively gratified as here.'

After the railway arrived in Margate in 1846, people came in their droves, convinced that a dip in the sea was something of a cure-all. The

LEFT: DESPITE EXTENSIVE
BOMBING DURING THE SECOND
WORLD WAR, CANTERBURY
CATHEDRAL'S STAINED GLASS
WINDOWS, WHICH DATE BACK
FOR CENTURIES, ESCAPED
TOTAL DESTRUCTION.

OVERLEAF: MARGATE WAS
A POPULAR DESTINATION
FOR TRIPPERS KEEN TO TAKE
ADVANTAGE OF ITS BRACING AIR
AND REFRESHING SEA WATERS
FOR HEALTH REASONS.

Royal Sea Bathing Hospital had already been established in Margate for 50 years, to provide swimming for the less well off. It was, however, an era before the concept of swimming costumes. For this reason there were bathing machines on hand to protect everyone's finer feelings.

Bathing machines were in effect wooden carts that could be hired by bathers. Getting into the machine on the beach, the swimmer would disrobe away from prying eyes. The machine was then propelled into the water, sometimes by hand but usually under horsepower. At the required depth the cart came to a halt and the bather dropped out, seaward side, to swim at leisure, usually naked. A bather indicated that his swim was finished by waving a flag to attract the attention of the machine operator.

Margate Quaker and glove maker Benjamin Beale (c.1717--75) claimed to have invented the bathing machine. In fact, it's likely that they adapted an existing machine by attaching a canvas awning at one end which could be pulled down to the water encasing the swimmer in a small area.

As the railways brought in day-trippers, the necessity for bathing machines became not only to keep men and women apart but also

THE NECESSITY FOR BATHING MACHINES BECAME NOT ONLY TO KEEP MEN AND WOMEN APART BUT ALSO TO SEPERATE THE UPPER CLASSES FROM THE MIDDLE CLASSSES

WHEN SWIMMING COSTUMES BECAME COMMONPLACE, BATHERS WERE RELEASED FROM THE CONFINES OF BATHING MACHINES WHICH WERE USED PREVIOUSLY TO SPARE THE BLUSHES OF NAKED SWIMMERS WHEN THEY ENTERED THE WATER.

to separate the upper classes from the middle classes and to keep both away from the workers. By the 1880s swimming costumes were being widely used, which diminished demand for bathing machines. However, they are frequently seen on postcards from numerous British resorts at the turn of the twentieth century and are thought to have been in sporadic use as late as 1927.

Five minutes' walk from the sea front is something else that Margate kept under wraps in the early part of the nineteenth century. The Shell Grotto was discovered under farmland in 1835 by James Newlove, who immediately set about making a commercial success of his discovery.

Since the first visitors descended into the grotto two years later the jury has been out about who built it and why. Inside there are some 4.6 million shells arranged in mosaics, patterned or depicting trees and symbols. These are not exotic shells imported from a far-flung beach, but the highly familiar ones from cockles, whelks, mussels and oysters.

But why go to so much trouble? Some people maintain that the grotto was a Regency folly, while others believe it to be a smugglers' retreat. The most recent theory is that it was a temple linked to sun worship. But no one knows for sure. Attempts to carbon date the shells have failed because they are covered with years of pollution given off by Victorian lamps which once lit the way for visitors.

Along the coast of fortress Kent are the Roman remains at Richborough, dating from the first invasion in AD43. Bradshaw tells the traveller to watch out for the site from the train as it heads across Sandwich flats past the hamlet of Saltpans. 'At this spot the memorable ruins of Richborough come fully into sight; and shortly after the train sweeps around the sandy hill on which they stand. This was a celebrated Roman station … the remains of an amphitheatre are still very apparent. In the centre of the great quadrangle is the celebrated prostrate cross, built to commemorate the introduction of Christianity into England. It is placed on the top of an immense heathen altar and marks the spot on which Augustin preached the gospel. No monument in the kingdom equals this simple cross in interest yet few have been treated with greater neglect.'

Of course, the departure of the Romans and the introduction of Christianity are separated by 200 years, but Richborough continued to be important long after the Roman settlements had disappeared, probably thanks to its key defensive position.

Less well known is the First World War port developed at Richborough from 1916, taking advantage of its rail links. Acting as a secret supply base and encampment, it was known as 'Q' and was the last that countless British soldiers saw of England before setting off for the trenches. On 10 February 1918 a cross-channel ferry began between Richborough and Calais, the first roll-on, roll-off design. A further 60 miles of track were also laid at the port for transporting locomotives and wagons with heavy guns and tanks to ships.

At the end of the war the port silted up and the camps which once held men preparing for war were deserted. The ferries, though, were taken to Harwich and began running regular services to Zeebrugge in the 1920s.

From Richborough the line continues south and reaches the coast at Deal. Here, according to Bradshaw, the railway helped to transform a notorious smugglers' haunt into a respectable Victorian seaside town. 'This town stands close to the sea shore which is a bold and open beach being defended by an extensive wall of stones and pebbles which the sea has thrown up. Deal was formerly a rough looking irregular sailor-like place, full of narrow streets and shops with multifarious articles termed slops or marine stores. It is however much improved and is now resorted to for sea bathing, especially on account of its good repute for moderate charges.'

A mile down the coast is Walmer Castle, built by Henry VIII to repel French and Spanish invasions. Although it dates from the 1530s, because of its circular keep it is often mistaken for one of the Martello towers built around the south and east coasts in the early nineteenth century as protection against a Napoleonic invasion. They took their inspiration and name from a rounded castle in Corsica that had defied the might of the British navy in 1794. Each of the 74 Martello towers was armed with a cannon. At Walmer Castle, in 1801, with Napoleon's great army encamped near Calais, poised to invade, Admiral Horatio Nelson discussed his plan of action with William Pitt.

Today Walmer Castle is the official residence of the Lord Warden of the Cinque Ports. This is the name for a confederation of towns that banded together for defensive and economic purposes perhaps as early as Norman times. (The towns were Dover, Sandwich, Hythe, Romney and Hastings.) Its wardens have included the Duke of Wellington, who died in an armchair there in 1852, Sir Winston Churchill, W.H. Smith and the Queen Mother, the only woman to have held the office.

RIGHT: **DEAL WAS ANOTHER KENT SEASIDE TOWN TO BENEFIT FROM THE ARRIVAL OF RAIL SERVICES. AN INFLUX OF VISITORS CHANGED IT FROM SMUGGLERS' HAUNT TO RESPECTED RESORT.**

OVERLEAF: **DEAL, PICTURED HERE FROM ITS PIER, OFFERED AMPLE OPPORTUNITIES FOR LEISURE SEEKERS.**

Deal did apparently witness one successful invasion. It is claimed locally that between the lifeboat station and the pier is the very spot where Julius Caesar first set foot on land in 55BC.

Today, in common with Greenwich, Deal also has its own operational time ball, the first to be operated by a direct signal via the railway telegraph.

Nearby Folkestone was also rejuvenated by the arrival of the railway, which makes a spectacular entry through carved cliffs to give passengers a stunning water's-edge experience. It was transformed from fishing village to cross-channel port after 1847, when the the South Eastern Railway invested in a new harbour that brought trade and tourism to the town.

Ultimately the railways brought the possibility of a channel tunnel into life. Talk of a tunnel dates back to 1802 when French mining engineer Albert Mathieu put forward his design. A year later, the first English design was proposed by Henri Mottray. But it wasn't until the 1880s that it became a serious prospect. Once again it was the South Eastern Railway putting up the cash. Although tunneling began, fears that the French would use it to invade prompted Parliament to put a stop to the project. Another attempt begun in the 1970s faltered for lack of investment.

The tunnel that's in operation today was started in 1988 and plunges some 75 metres below the sea bed. First used in 1994, it is an engineering feat of distinction. A desire to hold Europe at bay has by now been replaced by the economic necessity of reaching out to our neighbours. However, just as the canals suffered as the original railways flourished, the ports have taken a pummelling because of the cross-channel rail link.

Three miles west of Folkestone, and once served by a branch line through Hythe, is the beginning of another major line of defence. Between 1804 and 1809, when an invasion by Napoleon again seemed imminent, the Royal Military Canal was dug from there to Winchelsea in a 28-mile arc along the inland edge of Romney Marsh.

Meanwhile, as if to symbolise Kent's dual role, the very stretch of coast behind which the canal curves is now the site of one of the county's best-loved tourist attractions: the miniature railway that runs for 13 miles across the marsh. The brainchild of two wealthy racing drivers who were also railway enthusiasts, it was opened between Hythe and New Romney in 1927 and extended to Dungeness in 1828. One of its stations is at Dymchurch, where Edith Nesbit, the author of *The Railway Children*, was born, and where two Martello towers can be seen.

11220. - DEAL. VIEW FROM PIER.

The next part of the journey took us back to Ashford and off down a different line to the south-west. Perhaps inadvertently, while travelling on a similar route Bradshaw identifies a possible new industry for Kent. 'The main line on leaving Ashford makes a gradual approach towards the coast, swerving slightly to the south east and having on each side a delightful champaign [sic] country.'

Indeed, the chalk downs of the south coast are mirrored across the channel in the region that makes champagne. The climate is also similar. Now, for the first time, Kent is gaining a reputation for the sparkling wines it produces. Using Pinot Noir, Chardonnay and Pinot Meunier grapes, Kent's wine makers are winning international prizes for flavour, colour and bouquet. The amount of land devoted to vineyards has increased by almost 50 per cent in five years. By 2014 the Kent harvest is likely to produce at least 3 million bottles of still and sparkling wine.

The line from Ashford bridges the Royal Military Canal and heads across the western side of Romney Marsh and the Isle of Oxney and out of the county. Once in Sussex it again crosses the canal before reaching Rye. Like its neighbour Winchelsea, Rye was once a thriving medieval port and made an additional member of the Cinque Ports, but is now some way inland.

All enquiries to PR 300
Information Bureau, Hastings

HASTINGS
AND ST. LEONARDS

Fast and Frequent Service
of Trains from London

BRITISH RAILWAYS

LESS A BATTLEGROUND, MORE A PLAYGROUND, HASTINGS WAS TRANSFORMED WITH THE ARRIVAL OF THE TRAIN AND BEGAN CATERING FOR HOLIDAYMAKERS WHILE MAINTAINING ITS BEACH-BASED FISHING FLEET.

Our final destination on this journey is Hastings, whose name will always be associated with the last successful invasion of England. In fact it was six miles away, at what is now called Battle, that William the Conqueror defeated King Harold, but it was at Hastings that he prepared his forces for action after landing at Pevensey.

The most westerly of the Cinque Ports, Hastings too fell on hard times after its harbour silted up. However, early in the nineteenth century it became a genteel watering place. Then came the railway in 1851, and the town prepared itself for change. Bradshaw remarked approvingly, 'The openness of the coast and smoothness of the beach have long made Hastings a favourite and recommended resort. The shore is not abrupt and the water almost always limpid and of that beautiful hue so inviting to bathers … A very efficient substitute for a trip to Madeira.'

Today it is not the colour of the sea that catches a visitor's eye but the way the beach has been transformed into a boat park. Indeed, Hastings claims to have the largest beach-based fishing fleet in England.

The boats are pulled up after each trip on to an area of beach known as the Stade, which was greatly improved thanks to the building of a groyne and a harbour at the end of the nineteenth century to shield it from shingle movement. Fishing gear was traditionally stored in the net shops, unusually tall, narrow buildings coated in tar to protect them from the elements. Of necessity the boats must be small, and that means the system of fishing is guaranteed to be sustainable.

The south-eastern corner of Britain has evolved from keeping the rest of the world out to actively beckoning people in. Without doubt railways helped bridge the gap between the no-nonsense Napoleonic rebuff carefully constructed around Kent and beyond at the beginning of the nineteenth century to the breaking down of borders that has been taking place increasingly since the railways came on the scene.

Some 170 years after it was published, Bradshaw had again proved invaluable in guiding us on our journey through Britain. With it we'd marvelled at the extraordinary Victorian achievements, but also celebrated what's still so exciting about modern Britain. With the last of our journeys at an end and the team finally heading back to their homes, it was with surprising relish that our thoughts turned to where we could go next …

USING PINOT NOIR, CHARDONNAY AND PINOT MEUNIER GRAPES, KENT'S WINE MAKERS ARE WINNING INTERNATIONAL PRIZES

INDEX

PICTURE CREDITS

2 & 6-7 Photolibrary; 11 © Steve Peskett; 14-16 Photolibrary; 17 © National Portrait Gallery, London; 20-21 & 23 © Steve Peskett; 27 Maria Platt-Evans/Science Photo Library; 29 Liverpool Record Office; 31 Stapleton Historical Collection/Photolibrary; 32 Salford Local History Library; 35 & 36 The Art Archive; 39 SSPL/Getty Images; 40-41 Paul Thompson/Photolibrary; 43 Keasbury-Gordon Photograph Archive; 44 Wakefield Libraries/© Dunhills; 47 Flight Images LLP/ Photolibrary; 48 David Clapp/Photolibrary; 50-51 Getty Images; 53 © Tony Bartholomew; 57 Getty Images; 58 SSPL/Getty Images; 60-1 STEAM Museum of the GWR, Swindon; 64-5 Bath in Time - Bath Central Library Collection; 66 Photolibrary; 68-9 Getty Images; 70 © Science Pictorial /Science & Society; 71 © NRM - Pictorial Collection/Science & Society; 75 SSPL/Getty Images; 76-7 Photolibrary; 78-9 Francis Frith Collection/Photolibrary; 81 Getty Images; 82-3 © Jon Hall; 85 Art Archive; 86-7 Photolibrary; 89 SSPL/Getty Images; 94-5 Photolibrary; 100-1 John Smedley's Archives; 102-3 & 104 Ian Peaty's Collection/Brewery History Society; 106, 107 & 108 Cadbury UK Archives; 111 & 112 Getty Images; 114-5 © Steve Peskett; 117 © Transport for London Collection of London Transport Museum; 121 & 122 Keasbury-Gordon Photograph Archive; 125 © Michelle Waller/Cumbria Wildlife Trust; 126-7 © grough.co.uk/Alamy; 129 SSPL/ Getty Images; 130-1 © 2010 Cumbria Image Bank; 133 Stewart Smith/Alamy; 134 Photolibrary; 137 Getty Images; 138 Photolibrary; 140-1 Topfoto; 142 Ross Aitkin; 146-7 & 148 SSPL/Getty Images; 151 akg/North Wind Picture Archives; 152 Shropshire Archives; 155 © Alan Novelli/ Alamy; 156-7 © Mike Hayward/Alamy; 158 & 161 Photolibrary; 162-3 Francis Frith Collection/ Photolibrary; 165 & 166-7 Photolibrary; 169 Norman Potter/Rex Features; 173 Getty Images; 174 Scottish National Portrait Gallery, Edinburgh, Scotland/The Bridgeman Art Library; 176-7, 178, 180-1 & 182 Getty Images; 184 © Trinity Mirror/Mirrorpix/Alamy; 186-7 Photolibrary; 189 Photo © Christie's Images/The Bridgeman Art Library; 190 & 193 Photolibrary; 107 Institute of Civil Engineers; 198 Mc Dowell Trust Collection of the Stephenson Locomotive Society (Newcastle Centre); 199 Sybil Reeder; 200-1 & 203 South Tyneside Local Studies Library; 206-7 Library Of Congress Prints and Photographs Collection, Detroit Publishing Company; 208 Francis Frith Collection/Photolibrary; 212-13 The Sutcliffe Gallery; 214-15 Harrogate Borough Council; 216 E. Oldroyd and Sons; 223 & 224 Getty Images; 226-7 SSPL/Getty Images; 228 & 230-1 Getty Images; 232 The Sutcliffe Gallery; 235 Popperfoto/Getty Images; 236 SSPL/Getty Images; 239 Colman's Unilever Archives; 240 SSPL/Getty Images; 245 & 246 Photolibrary; 249 Getty Images; 250-1 Photolibrary; 253 Getty Images; 254 SSPL/Getty Images; 256-7 & 258 Getty Images; 261 SSPL/NRM/Pictorial Collection/Getty Images; 264 NRM - Pictorial Collection/SSPL